Financial Management in the Church

BEING STEWARDS OF RIGHT RELATIONSHIP

Peter Henrickson

ISBN: 1-4392-1054-3
ISBN-13: 9781439210543

Visit www.booksurge.com to order additional copies.

HERE'S THE WAY I SEE IT

FIRST, GET RIGHT IN YOUR HEAD

Articulate Your Principles 7
    Financial Policies – appendix 1 104
    Employment Philosophy – appendix 2 111

Look Ahead, Not Back **11**
    Healthy Program Services 11
    Determining Financial Capacity 12
    Gauging Unmet Needs 14
    Requesting Committee Plans – appendix 3 113
    The Vision Budget – appendix 4 114

Give Meaning to Membership **15**
    Service as Revenue 20
    Membership Standards Bylaw – appendix 5 115

Foster Generosity **23**
    The Budget as Hindrance 23
    The Vision Budget 27
    Embracing the Vision 32
    The Stewardship Drive 34
    Privacy 38
    Percentage Commitments 40
    Monthly Contribution Commitments 42
    Collecting the Monthly Commitment 43
    Budget Drive Calendar – appendix 6 117
    Giving Guide & Pledge Form – appendix 7 120
    Canvasser Guidebook – appendix 8 123

Three Stories, to sum it up **45**
    Story 1 45
    Story 2 49
    Story 3 52

ORGANIZING AND DOING

Funds: How many do we really need? . . . . Really? **55**
    Attractive Considerations of a Single Fund 56
    The Taxable Income Corporation 57
    Endowment Funds 58
    Endowment Fund Policies – appendix 9 126

Compensation Management **61**
    Employer Philosophy...61
    Distinguishing Employment Types 62
    Relating Compensation to Employment Type 64
    Holidays..65
    Annual Leave and Sick Leave..65
    Benefits and Retirement..66
    Compensation 67
    Personnel Policies – appendix 10... 127
    Wage Scales – appendix 11 140
    Recording Pay and Benefit Decisions – appendix 12............. 144
The Chart of Accounts: The key to getting useful information later....... **71**
    Chart of Accounts – appendix 13.. 148
Right Brain Accounting (with pictures!).. **75**
    How Accounting Works – appendix 14...................................... 153
    Consistency Is Key – appendix 15 163
Borrow to Build **81**
    Three Positive Reasons to Consider Using Loans 82
    Sources of Capital Funds 84
    The Capital Campaign 84
    Loans and mortgages – appendix 16 169

ANALYZING AND REPORTING
Internal Controls and Financial Oversight **87**
    Audit Procedures – appendix 17 171
Cash Management **91**
Reporting: Can we keep their eyes from glazing over? **95**
    Financial Reports 95
    Stewardship Reports 100
    Software – appendix 18 178
    Financial Reports – appendix 19 179
    Endowment Financial Reports – appendix 20 184
    Canvass Assessment – appendix 21.. 185

Finl Thoughts **103**

Bibliography **189**

WHO IS THIS FOR?

This is a book mostly about money in the church: getting it, using it, and accounting for it. I hope that church treasurers everywhere will find the effort helpful, and that some will feel emboldened to change the way they manage their responsibilities.

However, it is also about the way we join ourselves into a church, how we align with intention to be religious together. Money, with all the meanings we attach to it and with all the talking we do about it, is part of the bonding glue of our togetherness. Our treasurers function within the larger context of our beliefs and attitudes about money and membership; and, it is this attitudinal context that is at the core of what I address. There is some discussion about technique also, which those who do the day-in and day-out financial record-keeping will understand most readily. Thus, it will be helpful for all who are responsible for guiding our churches: those who serve on the finance committee, those who serve as trustees or deacons (or who may someday), and those who are pastors, ministers, or staff. While the book is based in financial thinking, it is for the entire leadership – whether financial stewards, spiritual stewards, administrative stewards, or buildings and grounds stewards.

As you read through the book it will become clear that I am a Unitarian Universalist, and I have written from that perspective. Earlier editions have been used and praised also by leaders in other denominations. As a consequence, I have made attempts to broaden the language I employ. Where my efforts are insufficient, I ask that you make further adjustments as you need them, in the belief that an open-hearted reading of the material presented here might be helpful in other faith communities.

I want to thank many who commented and cheered me along the way as I wrote and rewrote. Many with whom I have corresponded on the internet through "discussion lists" such as UU-money have forced me to defend or change my thinking during the last several years. Some of the material is simply an airing or expansion of their good thinking and I am thankful for their virtual assistance. At the other extreme my wife, Gretchen Meyer, deals with the flesh and blood of my presence: She puts up with my crabby insistence that I like the way I write while gently encouraging a more holistic and systemic view of church dynamics, greater clarity, and better use of commas.

K. Peter Henrickson
September, 2006

ARTICULATE YOUR PRINCIPLES

How many churches have both an annual budget drive and an annual financial crisis?

How many congregational leaders know the size of the current budget for their church --- within, say, $10,000? Or, the results of the stewardship drive supporting it?

How many church trustees understand the monthly financial report? How many can say (even in an "open book test" with the monthly financial report in front of them) how much is on hand for paying bills or how much remains on the mortgage?

Frequently such questions bring embarrassed snickers. The uneasiness with which we consider such questions is dreadfully familiar; we seem to have widespread financial ignorance and disarray, a low grade infection in the body politic that keeps leadership lethargic and in a continuous funk. So, we fanaticize: "If only we could get average monthly giving up to $150 . . ." Or, "If only we had 20 more members . . ." Or, if only we had an endowment . . ."

> *"We have met the enemy, and he is us."*
> Pogo

Recruiting wealthy members will not fix the problem; pleading for more commitment from the uncommitted is ineffective; an endowment of meaningful size will take many years to build and may detract from other giving. What is needed today is careful thought about the qualities that make a community healthy and whole, about Right Relationship. And, we need financial management practices to reinforce these principles. Rudimentary accounting and finance concepts can help secure the spirit of health we seek for our religious community.

"OK" you say, "I know money is important but do I really need to think about the church in those terms?" Yes! Money is neither the problem nor the solution; but, our patterns of thought about church finances give us insight into how we think about our church community. If the membership can see no programmatic progress in the budget, for example, it suggests that the leadership lacks vision. If we shelter the money of distinct groups, we reinforce a fractured, distrustful sense of our community.

Sound financial practices do not solve the problems of a congregation, but a lack of mindfulness creates barriers that can make existing problems intractable. So, if the suggestions offered here seem burdensome or irritating, it is more likely because of underlying and unexamined social norms than because of disagreement over accounting practices. In that spirit we need to state clearly how we intend to bind ourselves into a spiritual community. This is as true in finance as it is in ministry.

a) We need clarity of purpose in the present: We need to think about why our church community exists for individual members. What are they seeking? Most congregants give money to their church in exchange for something, to have something they value present in their lives. We need to know what it is to assure they are getting it.

b) We need a vision of what we want to be: Not all our purposes can be met fully this year. Some of them are worthy enough to pursue over a long time. That's our vision. A discriminating articulation of a shared vision helps the congregation set its priorities for today.

c) We need to work toward wholeness in the community: A congregation is a single entity, not a collection of separate interests. Our minds dissect the community so we can understand it, but that is not the nature of it. So, our financial practices need to foster trust in each other and in our leadership, rather than reinforce the premise that particular interests in the community ("my" interests) need protecting against the onslaught of others.

d) We need to support each other in our efforts to do well: A community depends on individuals carrying out activities in ways that are supportive of the life journey of others. Sometimes we pay people and call them "staff"; others get a pat on the back and a potted plant at year end — we call them "volunteers". They all deserve full and fair compensation of recognition for their efforts. No one should feel unappreciated by a miserly congregation.

e) We need to support our colleagues as excellent managers: Excellent management depends, in part, on clear financial information. If there are church leaders who do not understand the financial affairs of the church, change the format of the information they receive. This is more easily accomplished and is a more fruitful course of action than attempting to change the characteristics of the leadership.

f) We need to underscore the meaning of membership: A church is not made up of any who may stumble through the door. While we welcome diversity in our midst and take in the stranger, we must insist that *membership* is formed in expectations of communal support beyond that extended to those we chance upon at the bus stop. Each church community must wrestle with the meaning of boundaries for its own membership, yet surely our expectation of members includes supporting the principles and purposes we profess as a denomination. Surely our lives should manifest those principles and purposes by focusing our time, our energy, and our resources to bring our values to life, to our life.

g) We need generosity of spirit: It is part of our spiritual presence to be responsive to the needs of others. There are those in our churches who need more than they give, whether spiritually, emotionally, or financially. In truth, none of us is generous all the time. We each have moments of need. We practice a generous spirit while reminding ourselves of how we wish to be treated in our dark times.

The only way to have healthy supportive communities is to start today, and then to practice, practice, practice every day henceforth. As we master our practice the community becomes more peaceful, more manageable, more integrated spiritually and emotionally, and more energetic in its impact on the rest of the world. Such a community becomes attractive to new members as well as old, inspires commitment to Right Relationship and stewardship. This is the entire reason for our effort. It is a noble purpose.

LOOK AHEAD, NOT BACK

Most churches do not have enough resources to accomplish what the membership says it wants. The Community Congregation is no exception. The leaders of TCC believed part of the problem was they had not presented a clear statement about the future in which all could feel compelled by the church's role in their lives and in the surrounding community. At the annual retreat the Trustees decided on a long term planning effort in the following sequence:

a) Determine the program services that would bring the current church community into bloom, simultaneously outlining a budget adequate to that vision (while being neither austere nor excessive) and setting in place the programmatic seedlings which could be nurtured into the vision they dreamed of for five years in the future.

b) Estimate the congregation's financial "carrying capacity," the financial support levels that could be attained with a minimal expectation of 3% in average pledging with a goal for average pledging of 5%.

c) If there is unused carrying capacity, assist the congregation in identifying priorities for moving toward the vision.

Healthy Program Services

What is required at TCC initially is guidance for the congregation on what a state of sufficiency would look like within the context of current congregational services. It is not difficult to substantiate some general parameters.

TCC is a congregation with 187 supporting individuals or families, including 243 adult members, and 105 children in the religious education program. Programs are ongoing, but there is general agreement that they operate at an unappealing and constricted level. The current annual budget is $251,000 with stewardship gifts running at about $215,000. The Board asked the Finance Committee to help determine how much would be required to meet the current expectations of staff and committees.

	TCC Sufficiency Budget[1]
Minister	$ 85,000
Administrator	$ 35,000
Director, RE (part time)	$ 40,000
Music (part time)	$ 14,000
Custodian (part time)	$ 14,000
Personnel	$188,000
Program Expenses	$ 38,000
Denominational Support	$ 20,000
Building & Grounds	$ 23,000
Total,	$269,000

This budget is for the current congregation with its current array of programs. It does not move the congregation into the programmatic areas many members have long talked of. It reduces annoying shortcomings but does not inspire a commitment to greater gifts.

Based upon discussions with the staff and committees during the prior year budget process, the Program Council suggested to the Board that there are three major needs being unaddressed currently: 1) the religious education program, particularly for teens and young adults is staffed sporadically by volunteers and is inadequate; 2) the congregation is not actively involved in any community service programs, though individuals are of course; and, 3) the office space is crowded, cluttered and unwelcoming and the equipment is old and inefficient.

What this congregation needs is an increase in gifts of 50% or more.

Determining Financial Capacity

The next step in financial planning at TCC is to determine how much money is available within the congregational community, with generous but not unrealistic giving expectations.

Even approaching the question made some of the leaders nervous. They were concerned that by openly talking about increasing the level of giving significantly both existing members and visitors would be scared away. The Treasurer noted however that the US population constitutes 4% of all humans on earth, yet consumes about 40% of the resources. Within the United States, Unitarian

---

1 These numbers are not unrealistic, but they are clearly only for illustrative purposes. They can be, and should be, modified by the assumptions local church leadership can make. Most church boards would probably find, as this one did, that with a 10% increase in income the current service program would be reasonably healthy. Use this approach to talk with the congregation about "where we are now, and where we would like to be now".

Universalists have the highest per capita income levels of major denominational groups, and the lowest level of charitable giving.

"The issue" she went on "is not about being able to afford making gifts to the church or some other charitable cause, but rather about being willing (or not) to do it. It's a question of choice, of what one wants, not what is imposed. There are people in our community with the same income level facing the same high expenses and the same family circumstances as those in our congregation who spend 3%, 5%, even 10% of their income on their philanthropic interests. They are in other denominations. But in any case, they choose to spend money on their church (or other charities) instead of spending it on cars, plasma TV's and dining out.

"On a scale either within the US and Canada or measured against the rest of the world," she noted, "UUs are not poor and, rather than pandering to a sense of scarcity among some, we need to increase the commitment we all feel to sharing what we have. If we want to train our members to develop greater generosity, we need to talk directly with them about how that generosity can change their own lives in knowing they have changed the lives of others."

Some of the Trustees continued to be nervous in discussing higher commitment levels for the future. They spoke of a desire to protect members who are less well off from feeling they don't belong in the church. The Minister, however, suggested that the leadership think about an approach to pledging in which everybody will understand and be receptive to a message about their values and the ability of the church to help bring them to fruition. Then, within a general conceptual approach to stewardship expectations, it would be easier to decide whether further discussion of exceptions is necessary. The others agreed that worrying about exceptions without first agreeing on the general approach made little sense.

After a second evening of discussion the leadership decided that the best and fairest way to approach the membership about gifts would be to adopt a percentage of income as the standard expectation for voting membership. They agreed further that the standard of giving should be stated as a percentage range beginning at 1% of a family's monthly take-home income. The lower percentage levels would be available to those living in lower economic levels; families with more disposable income would be encouraged to move to the higher giving levels over time. (The "Giving Table" adopted by TCC is offered in Appendix 7.)

Having a standard to use, the Finance Committee and two long term leaders who know the members well proceeded to obtain a rough estimate of the congregation's financial capacity. They made conservative estimates of family income, in $10,000 step increments. Having gone through all the pledging families and sorted them into stacks by income level, they were counted out. These family and individual units were multiplied by the mid-point of the income range. (Thus, the 23 families with incomes in the $50,000 to $60,000 range have total expected income of 23 times $55,000, or $1,265,000.) The total income for all families was multiplied by 3%. This very low percentage was used because it seemed a conservative average commitment level attainable in a church which recognized that many members already made much higher gifts.

When the leadership completed the exercise, they found that they had a stewardship commitment capacity of over $375,000 — nearly 75% higher than current levels.

Gauging Unmet Needs

Armed with this knowledge, the leadership could talk with the members about supporting the entire congregational program through stewardship gifts, leaving all money from fundraisers, endowment income and so on for special projects and services. In fact, the long-talked about $200,000 remodel for desperately needed office and meeting spaces could be undertaken. The congregation could fully pay a 15 year loan at current interest rates and leave a great deal of money for expansion of long sought for programs reaching into the larger community.

Some of the members objected , of course, to borrowing this money and wanted to launch a "capital campaign" to pay for the remodel immediately. Others pointed out however that getting members to agree to commit 3%, 4%, or 5% of their monthly take-home, they must push the congregation pretty hard and could not in good faith launch a special "capital campaign" on top of their newly increased commitment. They argued that such an expectation would surely drive away many members.

The Treasurer pointed out that the 15 year financing plan was clearly possible and did not endanger the congregation financially. Even if no large gifts came in during the first years of the mortgage and even if there was no congregational growth, the mortgage could be absorbed if gifts from members increased to the desired level. She added that some members who were able to make large gifts initially should be welcomed to do so and such gifts would make the project even less risky. There appeared to be no need to pursue a special "capital campaign" or a higher stewardship standard than that already being discussed.

With that clarification the Board was relieved and thankful. It appeared that the full financing of the current church program as well as the remodel could be accomplished immediately with a generous but not unattainable stewardship expectation. It also appeared that the congregation could begin to move into an inspirational mode of thinking about its future.

GIVE MEANING TO MEMBERSHIP

One might wonder whether the story of The Community Congregation has any relevance to the churches we lead. What is the point of talking about 3–5% of income when 1% is so hard to come by from so many of our members? And, why do we need to focus so directly on financial commitment levels? Isn't the church about something bigger than the amount of money people give?

Yes, and often No. The church not only provides a haven for us in our wounded times and continuing support for us in our idiosyncratic ways, it demands that we grapple with the meaning of our lives. It is the place in which we are called upon to continue to expand the depth of our relationships — with others, with the world, and with ourselves. The pursuit of such growth is spiritual practice.

So, Yes! The church is about money: Most simply, and most profoundly. It is a predominant feature of what church is about — not because our church needs to get through the next payroll or repair the roof, however. A church's struggle for money is the struggle of its parishioners to have lives of meaning. We give money not to build a church but to transform lives, starting with our own. Such transformation cannot take place while we pursuit an acquisitive lifestyle, ignoring the enormous responsibility we face to repair the world we live in for following generations.

Church leadership must foster generous giving as a vehicle for personal transformation. Such gifts need to be part of one's life not for the next five years, but for the duration. Remodeling the religious education wing is not the reason for getting a congregation to increase giving levels. Rather, it is the mechanism — it is what we talk about. The reason is to bring lives of value into focus.

Having said this however I want to affirm that there are two schools of thought on how we should define membership standards to determine who should be able to vote and hold office. Some feel that everyone should be welcomed into community without reservation, and all who are welcomed should be confirmed the full right to participate politically. Others claim that a church community, like any other, has standards: whether doctrinal, financial, participatory, behavioral, or a combination of all. They argue that a healthy community considers its boundaries explicitly.

It is an important question for each congregation to address. There is no correct response – either can be a legitimate philosophical stand. It is a question of our spiritual practice, addressing how we wish to be in community.

What is not correct, in my opinion, is to answer the question with one spiritual stand while maintaining another political stand. If you argue that all who attend are included in community with equal rights of participation, for example, don't wail about how some people are not meeting your expectation of membership. If your philosophical or spiritual position requires universal acceptance of all voices, it also requires you to forego criticism of how they engage the community.

Nor is it appropriate for the congregation to agree that standards are important, but set them so low as to be meaningless to the member. The notion that a gift to the church of $100/year is sufficient for membership because it covers the costs of the newsletter, for example, fails to attend to any issue relevant to individual membership. The amount is set primarily to terminate a discussion members find uncomfortable. A meaningful binding of an individual in relationship to a church community has nothing to do with postage costs. Requiring cost recovery of the newsletter and denominational dues is a political response to a spiritual or ethical question. It is a compromise grounded in an interpretation of institutional needs (and an unreal interpretation at that); the issue of the individual's needs in establishing a relationship with the community in integrity is far more important — and is unaddressed.

> Why should one who dutifully pays a $100/year minimum pledge (and is employed) be included in a vote on whether to launch a capital campaign, or hire a second minister? That person is voting on how everyone but themselves should assume community financial burdens.

> Why should the person who cannot control their anger and screams at others during most business meetings be allowed to continue attending and voting? That person is disrespectful of the dignity of others, individual freedom of conscience, and the democratic process.

> Why should the Snowbirds who are no longer present except when visiting children at Christmas (and still pledge) be allowed to participate in the vote to Call a new minister? They are not present to witness the pastoral mess, nor to listen weekly to an uninspired service. It's not about the money.

I believe church life is foremost a calling to integrity. In part, it is a calling to integrity in our relationship with those around us. Everyone needs to engage the meaning of membership before having a voice in governance. The purpose of a church goes beyond scheduling potluck dinners for a bunch of folks who enjoy chatting. We are in church precisely because "church" is a place to forge particular relationships crucial to our identification and selfhood. All relationships have expectations built in; the parties must hold up their end of the bargain. Surely being in a church is not something we should embark upon while determining "what is the least I can do here?" Does anyone seriously argue that we practice the best of Unitarian Universalism when we hold ourselves out as the Church of the Least Committed? While all are welcome to drink from the community well, simply partaking of the water does not confer a seat on the Water Board.

We want to be part of something, not alone. In joining a church we throw our lot into the pile, sharing the good and bad that may come from our association with others because we sense that doing so will improve our own lives overall. In so doing we differentiate among our relationships. We are not required to accept everyone into our network of friends. We set boundaries as to what we expect, and what we require. We determine that there are individuals with whom we will not associate.

A congregation is no different. It too determines its membership boundaries. A wise congregation will tend to those boundaries carefully.

The church belongs to those who are serious about their daily practice as members, whatever form that practice takes. While the liberal congregation may encourage attendance and participation from virtually anyone who chooses to come, the governance and the direction of the community are the responsibility of those who invest their time, their person, and their money seriously. The questions which face a congregation, such as: "Should Reverend Jones be our pastor for the next several years? Should we build a new building here or move across town? Should we continue to allow a convicted child molester to attend our congregational gatherings?" ought not to be decided by anyone who happens through the door and puts $10 in the collection plate. Yet some congregations, by the absence of any other standard, allow these issues to be debated with equal standing by all in attendance on the day of the congregational meeting – the committed, the dabblers, the uninformed, and the ignorant.

In any reasonable notion of democracy there is a test of citizenship, a proving of one's rightful place in the community. Serious thinking about democratic process must delineate standards by which one might be found unworthy of participation. In the bylaws of the Unitarian Universalist Association this identity between membership and voting is recognized as follows: *"A member of a member congregation is any individual who, pursuant to its procedures, has full or partial voting rights at business meetings."* At the denominational level there is an affirmation of the linkage between membership and the right to vote, while relying upon the local congregation to establish criteria.

Many in our congregations easily confuse these discussions about membership by blurring the distinction between the term "member" when used to refer to those we welcome into our midst as fellow seekers on Sunday morning and when used to refer to those we entrust with the corporate governance of the church. Some argue that there is no distinction in these meanings; I argue they wish to avoid the hard questions of boundaries.

The issue facing the local congregation is not one of determining who is or is not a Unitarian Universalist; it is one of determining who is or is not a member of the congregation. "UU" and "Member" are not synonymous terms.

It is the right of the individual to determine their own particular religious beliefs within their understanding of what that means. Further, the individual must decide whether to join a particular congregation. We all know people describing themselves as Unitarian Universalists (my own persuasion) who choose, for whatever reason, to not meet the requirements a congregation holds up for membership, however minimal those requirements might be. There is no fault or shame in making such a choice. Such people are still welcomed warmly into fellowship with the congregation — *but not as voting members.*

In the absurd extreme, surely, we could set up a table at the mall on Sunday afternoon and simply ask those who pass by whether we should call a new minister, or whether we should launch a capital campaign. We can all quickly agree that "those people are not members!" But, would any of those people who happened to attend one service and enthusiastically "signed the book" be welcomed as a member at the annual meeting that afternoon? Where is the distinction made between a modest interest in the congregation and voting in the election of trustees, or being a trustee? Surely the distinction amounts to far more than walking through the church door once or twice.

Too often the argument over membership is cast solely as a financial discussion. Membership ought not to be entirely about money, though that is part of what every significant relationship struggles with. Money is the form our discussion takes because, in part, it is an easy way to avoid any deeper discussion about the integrity with which we approach others.

There are three areas of commitment that every congregation must struggle with in defining membership boundaries. I have not set forth clear lines of demarcation for these criteria because each community must discern the meaning of the general standards for itself. To know that we are confronted with "grey areas" in making important decisions does not mean that the decision can be or should be avoided. The decision will be difficult and controversial, but no less important. In each of the three areas outlined below we can all agree, I'm sure, that some behaviors are clearly on the far side of any reasonable standard for community membership. (In Appendix 5 you will find a sample bylaw based upon the following discussion.)

First, one must be present in the life of the congregation. One cannot be a "member" of any community without putting in time, without being present within it. In a church community one must attend services reasonably frequently, and/or one must participate in other social and service ministry activities of the congregation. There is no other way to know the people in the community. If one doesn't know the other people, one is not part of the community. Failure or inability to participate continually makes one a "friend" of the church, not a member. Those who disappear from life in the community should not be allowed to reappear at the congregational meeting several years later asserting their right to a voice in a sensitive or fractious discussion, even if financial support can be demonstrated in the interim. Such is only slightly less absurd than if one who has never attended and lives hundreds of miles away sends a check and asks to join the congregation.

Second, one cannot be a "member" of the church community without putting into everyday living the values affirmed in joining. One does not have to accept the Principles and Purposes of the UU denomination as creed to understand that one's life must be in harmony with them to be part of a UU community.

There are those in the world who we all agree do not abide by our Principles and Purposes, do not accept them, who we wish to distinguish from ourselves in our own living of life. Those others are "not members." The community can and should expect that all "members" will behave in ways that show respect for the inherent worth and dignity of all, for example, or the democratic process.

We each have edges where the Principles and Purposes get tested, where we keenly understand the relevance of them. Without affirming to live by them, an individual is not rightfully a "member" of a UU community. An individual can spend a great deal of time in the UU congregation and give a great deal of money and still fall short of the right of membership through continuing behavior that is blatantly offensive to the Principles and Purposes.

Third, we must rearrange our financial lives somewhat to include the congregation. Such rearrangement includes a fair measure of what flows to us. "Rearrangement" means that we recognize that we are all fraught with the vexation of difficult choices: college education savings, business expenses, remodeling the home, vacation, saving for retirement, school clothes for the kids, or fixed income. Becoming a member of a congregation means that the church too is high on the list of financial necessities. Because it takes a place on the list, it creates additional tension in competing for resources. But, being a "member" of a spiritual community requires that we look at our life as spiritual practice; we cannot always put beer and pizza and a trip to Cabo San Lucas ahead of our commitment to the church community.

The gifts we give to the church are not supposed to be comfortable, any more than putting money into a retirement plan is comfortable. Our gifts become spiritual when there is an element of sacrifice present in our sharing with others, when we require ourselves to rearrange our finances somewhat to make room for our church commitment.

Our gifts are not supposed to make us suffer either, however. Somewhere there is a balance. It is the job of church leadership to help the congregants find this balance in their lives. In any case, giving standards that we discuss within the congregation need to be based upon each individual's particular income level, rather than upon the notion that the individual must meet an arbitrary dollar need of the church.

Services as Revenue

There has been a long-running debate in most denominations revolving around whether the service that individuals perform in the church ought to be "service in lieu of money". Some contend that when we establish a requirement for monetary support before extending the right of voting membership, we invariably and unfairly discriminate against those less well off financially. To offset this "injustice," it is sometimes suggested that we also extend voting membership to those who volunteer for the many tasks involved in church life, and waive any expectation of monetary contribution for them. Clearly, both kinds of giving need to be held up and honored.

But, it's apples and oranges – kumquats and avocados. A good salad has both. Any truly important societal relationship makes independent claims on time and money. When I decided to get married and have kids, for example, I could not then claim that I can be a good father by devoting money to my children's' upbringing but not time – or because I spend evenings with them I do not need to provide costly health insurance. My commitment to raising a family is understood to place both money and time demands on me, and my obligations are not reduced simply by asserting that I have done enough in one arena to compensate for the other. My obligation to my church is not materially different in this respect.

Time comes and goes. We get to use it once. Sometimes we want to use it to enhance our lives. Sometimes we want to use it to watch "The Sopranos". Sometimes we would rather not go to the committee meeting at church because "The Sopranos" is on the same evening. We get to choose. How we choose is what we make of our lives.

It isn't simple. There are times when we would rather not be productive, or responsible. We just want to put our feet up and watch TV. But at the end of the month, most of us would rather be able to say we did something other than load up on soap operas and sit-coms. Finding something else to do with time makes us feel smart, kind, important, visionary, or whatever. It is what gives meaning to our lives. Giving meaning to one's life through the use of time is a given. Everyone decides or defaults.

Financial support of the church is what we do because we are part of a community which shares financial burdens. There is no default decision on financial support; we must choose. These burdens exist in the choosing of the relationship. Everyone in a community is expected to shoulder some of the burden, as they are able. It's about living with integrity. The weight of economic reality descends upon us all. And, every "price" inevitably excludes those who are unwilling or unable to pay it. Membership in our communities gets its meaning from commitment to healthy relationships, including nurturing gifts of both time and money.

Yet, every congregation also needs to establish a process to reconsider the unintended injustices of membership requirements. In many congregations the minister or a small committee of the Board will hear appeals from individuals and decide whether the normal membership expectations should be waived for any of a number of reasons. For most of our congregants, however, what is required is a reminder of why they joined the community, the importance of it in their lives, and their ability to make choices supportive of their membership.

FOSTER GENEROSITY

Imagine with me that one day I go to the animal shelter and get a couple of dogs to keep on my farm – because they are pack animals and need companionship. They are each only a year or two old and very rambunctious. I want to train them, but only in ways that are compatible with my values. My first training rule therefore is to support their right to a free and responsible search for Truth and Meaning. I will offer my dogs guidance but not give them "commands". Rather than telling them to "sit" or "come" or "lie down" I will say in a firm, clear voice "Be Good". They will determine for themselves what that means.

Then, when one of my dogs actually happens to come toward me or lie down upon hearing "Be Good" I will not say "Good Dog" or offer a treat. It is best to not make remarks singling out particular individuals for praise I think; it could bring on diminished feelings of self-worth among the rest of the pack. Each has inherent worth and dignity after all; raising one up for special treatment undermines valuing them equally, or might seem that way to others.

How long do you suppose it will take me to get my dogs trained, to change their patterns of behavior so that we can meet each other's needs and live together in peaceful community?

Every stewardship drive and every special appeal is fundamentally about getting people to change patterns of behavior. We are concerned foremost with ourselves and our families. Stewardship is about adding others to the calculus of decision-making. This requires some community discussion, community agreements about what we will strive for, affirmation of our individual efforts, and rewards for our successes. We need to re-think how we can promote generosity and stewardship in our churches – or nothing will change.

The Budget as Hindrance

Most church members engage in a depressingly familiar annual drive for sustaining gifts. First, the committees are given reports on how they have spent money in the past year and are asked to provide an idea about future requirements. Someone meets with the minister and staff to get an idea about what they will want next year. The Treasurer guesses how much income will come from monthly commitments, based on current membership and giving trends.

With all this input from different sources the Finance Committee (or, the Board in smaller congregations) adds it up, finds there is a shortage, cuts some of the requests, increases some of the revenue items, and comes up with a budget that is "balanced".

This budget is presented to the congregation which debates the proposal in an open meeting, often full of rancor over the various "cuts" or "waste" or the "lack of realism" in the revenue estimates. The budget debate focuses on the smallest expense categories, such as whether a second telephone line is really needed. At the end of the evening the budget is adopted, everyone goes home feeling upset and unenthusiastic.

This is how we kick off the annual stewardship drive.

What's wrong with this picture? I can think of four things; perhaps you see more. First, the process encourages the membership to consider their gift level as a function of how the church will spend money in the following year; we are supposed to become more motivated in our giving because we see that the church needs to have supplies, purchase insurance, and make retirement plan contributions. We do not engage this paradigm with other charitable organizations: Sierra Club, CARE, Planned Parenthood, Ducks Unlimited, and National Public Radio all receive our generous donations without our questioning their fiscal plans. We "know" what these organizations will do with our money, and we support them grandly in order that they can do more. The more generous our gifts, the more uplifted we feel as we become part of the force of good because the organization will do good for us, with us. While we are always concerned that our gifts be used wisely, we presume that the leaders (whom we often do not even have a voice in selecting) will continue to further our interests as they have in the past. Any church stewardship process initiated in consideration of a traditional budget does not foster a similar presumption.

Second, the process fractures the community as it squabbles over a "fair" allocation of resources, rather than bringing everyone together in support of diverse interests. This divisiveness seems almost intentionally generated as our perverse way of kicking off the drive to encourage sustaining gifts.

Third, the notion of a "balanced budget" is a paradigm which mistakenly leads members toward "zero sum" thinking – completely at odds with the reality of our communal enterprise. In the case of governmental agencies, for example, there is an estimated level of revenue within which the agency must live. The revenue usually derives from some tax base; and estimating it for the upcoming year is usually beyond the power of the agency to control. This reality contrasts quite strongly with that of church communities. In our churches the flow of revenue is, quite literally, by the design of the members themselves. The members of a church determine for themselves how much they will both provide and receive communally — how quickly they will fix the roof, hire the Youth Advisor, or set up the homeless shelter. Our relatively small and homogenous group is the only thing standing in the way of moving toward our dream.

Fourth, the focus is on tinkering with the spending pattern of the past, adjusting prior program patterns, rather than dreaming nobly of what can be in the future. We engage in patching up what we guiltily have left undone in the current year without much beyond a passing thought about where our fundamental path will take us three or five years from now. In truth, many members want the leadership to "not change things much around here; just do what we are doing already, but better".

In thinking about our stewardship efforts in this way, we can begin to see that there are two approaches to raising money in churches. One is "rationalistic." It is a paradigm in which we look for reasons for giving that are embedded in a budget which will improve on what we know now. It looks for stewardship commitments designed to satisfy demonstrated spending requirements. It looks for evidence that budget items have "met the test" by being examined and trimmed appropriately. It looks for reasonableness in the use of funds, usually in comparison to the past year with particular examination of any increases.

The other approach we might refer to as "visionary" or even "spiritual." A visionary paradigm asks that we call forth our own dreams for the future and makes us instrumental to their realization within our church community. This approach to seeking gifts does not look to an annual budget as the basis for giving. Spiritual giving asks instead that we wrestle with our own internal devils, examining our attitudes about scarcity versus abundance in our lives; that we embrace generosity and gratitude as an approach to living; that we consider the notion that we are in a lifelong relationship with our church community, much like marriage, in which continual performance appraisal is detrimental. It sees open-hearted devotion of time, money, and energy as part of the spiritual practice of melding oneself into relationship with a community of faith and values.

The devotion of most people is to rationality, undiminished particularly as it relates to giving away money. The rational approach to the church stewardship drive, however, is a way of continuing in a place of spiritual stagnation, for "wrestling with the devil" has always been hard work. In my own denominational history the fixation on finding a reason for making gifts to our church may arise out of our humanist traditions. Or, it may be that an entire generation of "come-outers" (in which so many have left the faith tradition of their parents) is frightened of anything that seems to take us back to an unpleasant childhood context. Or, perhaps the generation of "boomers" only understands money as a medium of exchange and cannot turn loose of theirs without a clear understanding, even agreement, about what is coming back.

All of these have been offered as explanation. Of course, it does not matter which is the more accurate causal statement. The result is clear: Unitarian Universalists have the highest incomes of any major denomination in the U.S., and the lowest percentage level of stewardship both in our churches and in charitable giving generally. We are not effective in inviting generous behavior. Perhaps we should change our perspective.

It is helpful here to think of people as falling into either of two groups: those with a wage earner mentality, and those with an entrepreneurial mentality. Wage earners understand their income as regular, predictable, limited. Wage earners get a paycheck and pay their bills. Life, for the wage earner, has inflexible income boundaries; planning starts from that reality.

The entrepreneur has a different reality. The entrepreneur decides first what it is that is to be attained, and only then begins to work on what is necessary in getting from the present to the future. Income, for the entrepreneur, is not fixed; it is one of many variables to be managed in bringing a vision into being.

Unfortunately, most of us are wage earners, and it is difficult to acknowledge and move beyond that frame of reference. Our churches, however, are small entrepreneurial enterprises that can be shaped and grown to be whatever we jointly decide to make them. It is helpful to imagine our financial process from an entrepreneurial perspective.

For example, we might spend more time creating a widely held vision of how we want to be in community together three to five years from now, of what our community would include if it were whole and healthy, of how we could respond to a doubling in size. Such an envisioning process requires an understanding of our individual place in the community which is quite independent of the particulars of spending in the next year. This is spiritual work.

The annual stewardship drive, then, would not seek justification from a budget. Rather, stewardship arises out of our common vision and the budget becomes a description of our first steps down our path together. It is a policy statement about community values. Everything we present to the congregation prior to the drive must be directed to one purpose: to make it easier for congregants to feel generous and supportive toward the community. The sole purpose of the vision budget is to inspire the community, not to control future spending. Our vision budget must light the path ahead to our communal gathering place.

We want to know, for example, that the congregation agrees that it wants a minister in the future, or an associate minister. We want to know that our staff will be supported with compensation packages that are both competitive and fair. We want to know that the community supports the development and training of both paid and volunteer staff. We want to know that the carpets will be cleaned and our building will be painted when needed without creating a financial crisis.

Behind our efforts to describe our community of the future, there is the notion that financial stability can be achieved, that we can attain a level of giving which adequately supports the desired service level. Increases in spending beyond this level come from additional growth in membership rather than additions in the average pledging level.

The Vision Budget

Let's first agree that there are different ways to present a budget. The two most common are referred to as the "line item budget" and the "program budget". Each of these formats works well depending upon the organization's dominant need.

Large organizations, particularly government agencies and large non-profits, need control and accountability over current spending. Voters, elected officials, unions, trustees, managers and stakeholders all ask: "How did the money get used? Was any of it spent inappropriately? How can we limit the amount paid for salaries?" The parties need to be answerable to each other on such questions. In such organizations "program budgets" have never gained traction because they do not address the organization's financial questions. The Finance Director is more pressured to answer "Why are we having cost overruns on that grant?" than the question "How will we cover the increased costs of this initiative in five years?" Both questions are asked; only one involves job security.

Churches and most non-profits are smaller, and more homogenous. The interests of the constituents are not nearly as diverse. While controls in small organizations are usually more informal, they are also probably more effective; current spending is questioned less, despite the occasional budget arguments. Issues of control take a second seat to issues of meaning and mission. The most important financial questions facing small not-for-profit organizations are "What are we about? What do we need to do? And, "where is the money coming from to do what we need to do?"

It may be in your church that accountability is the most important issue facing the congregation. While I readily admit that I have sat in on many discussions about newsletter costs being too high, such questions are not the greatest concern of the board. More often, the dominant issues center on raising more money so that we can better support our ministry.

A "line item budget" shows how much will be spent on postage, supplies, coffee, copy paper, and so on. This is boring stuff for which no one will increase their monthly commitment. How should we change? What is needed is a budget which will inspire donors to give.

The annual stewardship drive and the interlaced process of determining what services will be provided should be understood as a classical marketing effort. This does not diminish its purpose. "Marketing" the church involves asking members to focus on their thankfulness for the community relationship they have, on what they want additionally in that experience, and on the possibility of enhancing their lives through an expansive selflessness arising through the worthwhile collective enterprise of their religious community.

The process of creating a vision that is more than a year or two away is one of the most difficult tasks facing church leadership — ministers, boards, and committees. While we might appreciate the notion of having a widely shared long term vision for our community, none of us know very well how to temporarily set aside the problems facing us now in order to focus on another time. If one of our committees has a long term plan, we do not know how to support it. We worry about being dictatorial over the specific proposals that someone doesn't like; or, we get caught in a never-ending process of seeking complete consensus before committing the congregation to one course or another. Finally, once committed, we are too easily persuaded to revisit the issue three years later because the congregation is "different now".

I do not know any easy way to change the entrenched attitudes which tell us to focus on the present. We reduce expectations for programs and services because some (usually unnamed "others") in the congregation do not want future spending to increase. We hide expense items because of a fear that the community will not be respectful of some program.

Nonetheless, I know that whatever vision is adopted by a congregation becomes a vision only because of the leadership. A widely held and sustaining vision never arose out of the congregation without active nurturing by the few most committed over time. Such work is not done except by those who are the Board, the committee chairs, the ministers and the stalwarts of the annual stewardship drive. Vision simply does not happen if the leadership waits for it to arise from the pews. Here is a process that may help the leadership in your church get started:

o   Ten months before the beginning of the next fiscal year, the board of trustees should discuss the context within which they want the budget prepared. By this I mean, the Board should set forth its own notion of expected growth patterns, expected trends in giving, and other matters that could impact on the resources available or the demand for additional services.

o   These planning parameters get communicated to the committees and staff.

o   Six months prior to the new fiscal year the staff and the heads of the major committees should get together for general brain-storming. Each gets an opportunity (and has a responsibility) to say what changes they hope for over the next five years. This discussion is an opportunity for synergies to be explored and complementary program operations to be articulated.

o   Each staff person or committee head goes back to the smaller group they work with to develop the ideas in greater detail and to draft a three year budget projection.

o   Ideally, four months prior to the New Year the committee heads and staff get together a second time to share their specific budget ideas.

o   About three months prior to the new year all the individual budget pieces have been submitted and put into a decision-making format for the board. I prefer to prepare a "base budget" designed to carry on operations only as we currently know them. This base budget is usually slightly larger than the current budget by the amount of inflation, minor adjustments correcting obvious errors, and uncontrollable changes.

o   Then, a separate listing of all the new programmatic items is developed for the board. The board places these incremental additive items into three groupings: high priority, meaning those items which are necessary to sustaining the ministry and the staff; medium priority, meaning those items which will advance the ministry; and low priority, meaning those items which can be deferred without jeopardy or can be financed through special sources. A dollar cost is assigned for each item.

o   These general priority groupings give the leadership and the members a focus for what the current budget drive needs to achieve the program goals.

o   After the completion of the annual budget drive the Finance Committee can also make a reasonably accurate assessment of where the current year spending will end. Based on these two key pieces of information, it is fairly easy for the Board to finalize the budget for adoption by the congregation.

By whatever planning process is appropriate in your church the Finance Committee needs to showcase a set of targets for congregational services for three or four years into the future. The presentation of such plans and their longer term financial implications shifts the congregation's attention from considering the spending request for next year to considering where the congregation is heading. During the stewardship drive there is an opportunity to meld the conversation about congregational direction with the conversation about individual dreams.

I do not know that any particular process will always result in a congregational vision of itself for the future. I believe strongly however that such planning needs a catalyst to start it, and support by leadership to carry it to fruition. Even processes that seem to involve the "entire congregation" are successful only when the leadership is energized by the plans and focuses attention on them over a long time. A vision budget will help to retain the focus of the leadership. So, here are some guidelines for presenting a vision budget. (See the sample budget in Appendix 4.)

1) **Summarize and focus expenses into the major areas of energy for your congregation.** We want the membership to "own" the vision – to believe it is good and to love it passionately. Suppose we organize a vision budget around the major growth needs driving the church.[2] Consider these examples:

   Worship, Spiritual Growth and Exploration
   Organizational Services and Leadership Development
   Community Presence and Denominational Support
   Pastoral Support and Membership Growth

   These categories represent what is sometimes referred to as a "mission budget". They virtually scream out the necessity to describe why we are in community.
   The minister and board need to provide inspiring leadership in each of these areas — to show in greater detail the aspirations for your congregation. "Worship, Spiritual Growth, and Exploration", for example, might mean a year around ministry for children or additional emphasis on laity ministry. It might mean developing four or five regular services each week, each targeted to a particular group of people.

2) **Present a vision budget which is adequate to the community.** Too often churches limp along without the ministerial or other staff support they need, without an annual installment on the building repair fund, or without

---

2 See Loren B Meade's "More Than Numbers, The Way Churches Grow" referenced in the bibliography. I recommend it for further development of these notions.

sufficient funds for religious education supplies. Good leadership presents a vision budget to focus attention away from the discouraging present and toward the place we want to be within the foreseeable future.

I do not believe that any congregation can say with integrity that it enjoys a fullness of spiritual meaning in all of the four areas of energy suggested above if the average giving level is below $100/family/month. This represents a commitment approaching 2% where congregational monthly incomes average $4,000 to $5,000. The vision budget needs to show what the church could be with a growth of gifts to the 3–5% range.

The presentation of a vision budget should bring forth excitement about the opportunities facing the congregation. Develop the vision budget to get both the board and the committees to share their observations and their dreams. They are the core of the congregation and their common purpose for the future is building community.

3) **Include a multi-year forecast.** The purpose of a forecast is to show that the leadership has heard what the members want, that such a church is available in the future although perhaps not next year. Members understand that programs take time to launch; they need to see movement toward objectives. They will support growth with a vision that fits their own, that enhances lives today as it moves toward tomorrow.

Most of what your membership envisions will be championed by the various committees. Give committees a way to talk about why they do what they do, and how they want to do it better. Ask "How do you see your area of interest in three years when the committee is fully operational and we have "xxx" members?" In the development of the budget ask people what they want. Ask members "Why did you join? How are we doing? What is still missing for you?" (See Appendix 3.)

4) **Show the number of members or giving units currently and into the future.** Growth is important in most congregations, and the vision budget should elevate this discussion. This is also a way to focus attention on growing average stewardship levels. One might show average commitments separately for "members" and for all other contributors as a way of communicating the higher giving levels expected of membership.

5) **Put the entire budget on a single page.** Leave lots of white space on the paper and do not reduce the type size. When you have done this, you have a budget that is comprehensible to those not familiar with it. Again, the sole purpose of the vision budget is to increase the level of giving. We who are church treasurers often lose sight of this objective. We default to thinking the purpose of the budget is to present numbers, and more is better. In the vision budget, fewer is better.

6) **Do not show the congregation numbers with more than four digits.** The membership will not absorb numbers with length, or at least not an entire page of them. A budget totaling $150,000 - $250,000 can express $435 as ".4" while a budget of $500,000 should round to even thousands.

7) **Show the congregation a budget which addresses general program concepts, not committees.** The funds provided to the church are never the property of a particular committee. As much as possible keep everyone focused on the entirety of the community. A program area showing where the congregation is headed with "spiritual growth for children and youth" is better than having a budget with a line for "Religious Education Committee." Even if a program area is the responsibility of a particular committee or staff person (and it probably should be), do not use the committee name in presenting the budget to the congregation.

Embracing the Vision

1) **Have the membership "endorse" or otherwise embrace the general priorities suggested by the vision budget.** After all, we want to focus attention on the future. Some churches ask the congregation to adopt the annual budget. As you might guess from earlier discussion, I believe this can become an unhealthy frame of reference for the congregation if it is very detailed. If the congregation is to adopt a budget, offer one at a high level of generalization and stretching more than a year ahead.

2) **Be forthcoming with details if asked.** It should be clear that the one page vision budget is not an attempt to hide anything from the members. When you present the budget at the congregational meeting, have the detailed numbers available. You can even have some copies of the detail with 10 – 15 pages stapled together. Most people do not want to be confused

with this much detail; but have it ready for the quantitative types who are not yet on the Finance Committee.

3) **Give the membership a chance to do the right thing.** It is important that the leadership not make large cuts in a budget before presenting it to the congregation. (The committees are not asking for tobacco subsidies!) Proposals from committees are the explanations from members of our own community about how they want to be in service to us. The effort to put that before the congregation should not be quashed.

Too many of our members have worked in large bureaucracies in which the financing ethic is entirely different. Do not succumb to the notion that the Board is "not doing its job" unless it reduces the requests. The first job of the Board is to raise the resources necessary to make congregational programs successful. The same groups that have put forth their plans for the future are the ones which need to be inspired to finance them. Most experts in the field of church finance agree: It is easier and healthier to help the congregation increase the level of gifts than it is to cut programs. On the other hand, if a little paring back in the first year will produce an aura of a "consistent overall approach" or a "longer term growth curve" small adjustments are usually not offensive to anyone as long as the program is intact in the present and vigorous in the longer view.

4) **Use the vision budget to present real issues about the future of the congregation.** The budget for Community UU Congregation shown in Appendix 4 calls upon the community to extend its ministry both to a nearby retirement community and to the local junior college. This budget gives a focus for open discussion and the possible adoption of a shared vision that will endorse or reject such plans.

5) **In presenting the budget, do not undermine the message of stewardship:** *We are committed to this community of religious freedom and spiritual growth. We freely and generously support our congregation and all the basic programs that make it worthwhile.*

When presenting the budget for adoption every special fee shown such as the extra add-on fee for religious education registration, the adult workshop fee, coffee donations, or even infant care can be interpreted as failure of the congregation to support itself in a straightforward manner. The same is true of revenue from special events such as an auction night where such income is necessary to obtain a "balanced budget." When a vision budget is presented showing an ongoing heavy reliance on such items, isn't this a message projecting failure even before we start?

Passing the collection plate for additional basic support of the church can be understood as a message of stewardship failure.[3] Some of my bedrock Christian friends tell me the "bucket" (not "plate" mind you) only gets passed in their church for mission work. The routine support of the congregation comes in the mail like a monthly bill. I think they have thought this through more carefully than we. Many churches that have begun the practice of "giving away" the Sunday collection to other designated groups find the practice carries over to effect generous impulses during the annual budget drive.

Fundraisers are an excellent way to show off the community to potential new members. They are also a great deal of work and require the strenuous efforts of many people over a long period. My personal preference (and I think it makes pragmatic sense too) is to not rely on such activities in the basic annual budget, but rather to fund basic programs through direct contributions. The energy for organizing a fund-raiser will be more forthcoming, as will the cash, if it is for some special purpose. For example, take the support of the Transylvania partner church or the local AIDS project out of the budget, and take the auction revenue out too. Say in a budget footnote that the Board expects the congregation will hold this worthwhile fundraiser, not for the church but for the important mission of the other organization.

The Stewardship Drive

We solicit people in the church community not to get their money, but to help them actualize their dreams for the church community. People give money to the church to realize something about themselves, something they see expressed within their beloved church. As their friends and supporters *we have a duty* to help them articulate what they want. When we approach another member of the congregation to ask for a commitment of support we must understand our role as pastoral at its core. One of the most serious conversations one can have with another member is helping them imagine how their dreams fit within the life of

---

3 Note too that IRS rules make it increasingly important that churches verify all cash contributions.

the congregation. The annual stewardship drive is an opportunity to help those we love reconnect with the meaning and purpose of their lives.

In earlier editions of this book I counseled leaders to do the stewardship drive well (by which I meant intentionally) but that no one form of a campaign was superior to another. I was wrong, or at best sloppy, in making such a statement. I was blind to some of the more crass approaches to stewardship used in some churches. There are decidedly inferior formats in the context of the purpose stated above, and doing some forms of a budget drive "well" does not save them from predictably dismal results.

Some church leaders develop an attractive brochure and mail it with a giving commitment card, requesting that each parishioner complete the enclosed postage paid card and return it in the mail. Short of not conducting a campaign at all this is probably the most inappropriate of all approaches. Consider the subliminal message in such a request: "We really don't want to know you any better. Even in this most intimate request for your support of our programs we are not much concerned with how you feel about the congregation right now. You are, at the most fundamental level, not very distinguishable from others. You are a source of funds, little else. While we hope you will contribute, why you contribute and how much you contribute are of no concern to your church leaders."

You may or may not get a card back after having mailed it out; if you do, it will probably not include an increase. The implied request of a stewardship drive mailer is that the members continue in their existing relationship within the community, whatever form that takes — and this is the most predictable response, even if the brochure is printed in color on glossy paper.

Slightly better is the campaign that follows up the attractive mailing with a telephone call. A phone call is a step closer to personal contact — okay, a big step closer — but it still lacks sincerity. For example, when you call you do not know whether this person has other things on his or her mind. Even if you ask, chances are they will interpret this call for what it appears to be, an effort to get this distasteful job out of the way with as little involvement on your part as possible. Further, when a solicitor telephones a household with two or more members the conversation generally includes only one of them.

A positive stewardship drive will usually involve the intimacy of some form of face to face meeting. This should be accomplished privately. Meet in their home, have them come to your place for dinner, take them out for coffee. (Never solicit important commitments during coffee after the service or in the parking lot!) Or, it can be done through small group dinners. If the small group gathering is the selected vehicle, include the minister, the Director of Religious Education, or a trustee. Then, the minister can preach after the drive is completed on "What We Learned about What You Want".

In thinking about organizing face to face commitment meetings, understand there are four levels of givers among our congregants, and they each need to be treated differently. While it may be possible to gently move someone over time from one level up to the next, in general members will not be responsive and may be angered if they are told they should have a set of motivations substantially different than those they have already settled into.

1) Some people are **PRESENT** to support the church and what it stands for, but not as a major expression of their own life priorities. They are uninvolved in the life of the congregation beyond Sunday attendance, if that. Their giving tends toward a standard of "What is the least I can do that is still respectable and gives me some measure of standing in the community?" These people will pay the commitment all at once or in a few payments over the year. Their gift will not be a financial burden to them. They are not always the lowest givers – some make above average gifts, although giving will be less than 1% of their income. They are unlikely to increase their giving without a direct, personal reason. The Vision Budget described earlier will have little meaning for them, though it may if it is discussed as part of a personal visitation.

2) A **CONSUMER** wants to give a "fair" amount based primarily upon what they see others doing, or what they see as the cost of what they "consume" by their membership. They can be motivated to increase if they understand that "other people just like them" give more. From a spiritual point of view this is the most difficult group to deal with. They think of themselves as reasonably decent people who are part of the congregation. Unfortunately, they require an extended effort at changing their perspective to a more complete understanding of the purpose of the church. The consumer perspective is very self-centered. Their growth within the community requires that they develop generosity as an end, rather than giving instrumentally to serve their individual needs.

3) The next group is very supportive of the church, want to be **CONNECTED**, want the congregation to be healthy and want to feel that they are an important part of the community. They will be highly motivated by a Vision Budget showing where the congregation wants to be in three to five years.

4) Finally there are the **COMMITTED**. They are wedded to the congregation. They receive a major part of their life's meaning already from their involvement and support of what the church is doing. They will generously supply what is needed to further the church vision — if it is made clear and if they feel listened to in shaping it.

It is best if you can form groups of members with similar or compatible motivations when asking them to converse with each other about their gifts. Here are a few other guidelines for the face to face stewardship drive:

1) Every gift commitment must be followed up with a personal written note from either the minister or the board president thanking the person(s) and naming the amount. There is nothing wrong with the solicitor sending such a note too.

2) If your membership definition includes teens as members, they should be approached about their stewardship gifts separately from their parents. Every member needs to know what membership entails.

3) No single solicitor should be asked to conduct meetings with more than five persons; even if they complete their five and volunteer for more seven is the absolute maximum.

4) Never send a "consumer" or someone who is only "present" in the congregation to ask about the stewardship intentions of a highly committed contributor. It is offensive. In fact, don't ask anyone who is only "present" to solicit any others in the stewardship drive. Working in the stewardship drive is not a motivational tool for boosting the involvement of those who are only present.

5) If there are not enough stewardship leaders to cover the entire congregation with private face to face meetings, concentrate the effort on the those you believe are among the connected and committed. Work down from there. Use a less intensive venue for those remaining. Everyone who has been a member for less than two years however should be treated as though they have the capability and interest to become connected.

6) If someone cannot see a way to fulfill their stewardship desire with money, suggest alternative ways to donate (not services). For example, have the

library committee develop a list of needed books. The person can commit to scour the used book stores to try to find at least three or four during the year. Or, have them agree to bring snacks for the RE program six times during the year. Everyone needs to be relied upon.

Finally, you may want to conduct a Celebration Sunday in place of the face to face visits. It takes every bit as much work in planning over several months. Because it is an entirely fresh format for the congregants however, it can bring about renewed excitement and commitment to the congregation.

I have included a stewardship drive planning calendar in Appendix 6 and a sample guide that could be given to every canvasser in your stewardship drive in Appendix 8.

Privacy

Recognition of those among us who are most generous runs against the grain in many churches. When it comes to church giving we seem to think people should give money solely because of other-worldly motivations, unrelated to here and now societal connections. Secrecy in giving practices is the most powerful force strangling generosity in religious communities.

Think about my dog training program and why it won't work. We all know that training pets is a process of setting forth expectations and then consistently praising the desired behavior when it happens. We know that rewarding outcomes is more effective in getting the behavior repeated than inattention, punishment, or shame. This is what we know about pets and changing their behavior to make them more desirable. We offer clear signaling of expectations, and clear rewards for meeting them.

I assert as a father (and not as a child psychologist) that the same process holds true for children. We may (or may not) feel a little more sophisticated when we train our children and do not like to think of it in the same context as training pets. Yet, when pressed, we admit that the process of learning and socialization is remarkably similar. We show children a lot of love; we tell them what we want them to do; and, we reward them with more love and praise when they behave in ways we wish. This approach to child rearing is "good parenting." Consistently ignoring a child, whatever the behavior, is understood by most as "bad parenting."

Finally, when I look at the adult world I see indications everywhere that the same generalization applies again. People of all ages are more willing to change their behavior or engage in a difficult series of behaviors when an appreciation by others, commendation, or title accrues through such efforts. One might say "But, adults are not like children; they are mature." Meanwhile we strive for letters after our name (and display them); we seek promotions; we covet the symbols of well-being; and when our affinity group is recognized in the press, we proudly hang the picture and story on the wall – as though it says something about *us*.

All of us, no matter our age, respond readily to praise and recognition. We want to be known by our good accomplishments. We will do more to make ourselves Good People if others, in fact, have an opportunity to witness our goodness. We respond positively to praise and recognition no less than our Golden Retriever, although perhaps more subtly.

One might still argue that the real rewards of a well-lived life are going to be shown to us in the Hereafter. I do not dispute the possibility, even though I do not share that view of eternity. The rewards we know and respond to most predictably are those that come to us in this lifetime. My religion tells me to focus on the lifetime I am in, and to let the Hereafter take care of itself.

So, if we are trying to change people's beliefs and behavior about their own generosity it makes sense that we would use the same proven methods that we apply in other areas of life. We should not, for example, spend our time and energy focused on the poor performance of the lowest level of givers, preaching shame or damnation. Rather, we should recognize generous behavior whenever and however it occurs and hold it up as a positive example for others — frequently and consistently, just as we do for pets and children. Trying to train a pet or child in the absence of any reward system seems futile. Similarly, it makes little sense to try to change giving patterns in a church community without identifying and heralding with our love those among us who already demonstrate a generous spirit.

Of course, the church leadership can continue to conduct stewardship campaigns shrouded in complete secrecy — but don't expect behavior to change. Secrecy of giving and praise of generosity cannot co-exist. Yet many church leaders are set in the notion that all generous giving should be kept secret. When questioned about why, and not accepting the various versions of "that's just the way we do it around here" the response is frequently "some people might be embarrassed." Or alternatively, "It's just nobody's business."

Embarrassment or shame arises out of the strong incongruity between the self we hold out for others to admire, and some actual behavior we engage in which is different. When our behavior is seen to fall short of the image of ourselves we display, we are embarrassed.

Part of what we are about in religious communities is living lives of integrity — claiming values as our own and applying them in our daily living as consistently as we can. This integration of one's values and one's manifest life patterns is healthy religious work. Church leaders have a responsibility to help parishioners define what they value and then to live consistently within those values. It is quite appropriate that some people choose to not embrace the church as much as the devoted do. What we want to overcome is allowing anyone to claim he or she values the church community highly (and is entitled to a weighty opinion about its affairs) while adopting parsimonious and irresponsible giving patterns.

The argument that it is nobody's business when others are generous is also strange. We are supporting our staff, facilities, and programs as a common endeavor. It is our business — our communal religious business. When individuals stand out in their contribution of time or money we need to know and appreciate what they are doing for all of us. Stated or not, people expect something in return for their contributions. They certainly deserve well-evidenced respect by the leadership of the congregation.

How should we reward generosity? Send a thank you note in response to every stewardship commitment as a starter. Follow up the stewardship drive with public recognition of all those who make a commitment, perhaps especially noting those who increased the most from the prior year or those who are most generous within their means. Many churches list giving levels, such as Stewards and Benefactors. Recognize those who are most supportive in giving with special social invitations, or opportunities to participate in small group discussions where they are asked for their advice. Do not leave the most supportive members of your congregation wondering if they are alone, unknown in their efforts, and chumps for that.

In addition, throughout the year bring forth the names of those who have taken on some extra service responsibility, or have donated heavily toward a special appeal. Recognition should be slightly more public than the donor will initially be comfortable with. Those who are at the highest giving levels should be invited to a dinner or dessert with the minister. This is yet another chance for the leadership to talk with those who are most committed to the future of the community about what can and should be the future of the church.

Percentage Commitments

It is time let go of a "minimum" dollar expectation from each member. Too often congregations extend voting membership to those who give no money to the church; or, a congregation will accept "any recognizable gift". If a minimum is set, it is on the basis of the church's "marginal costs" of membership (for example, denominational dues plus newsletter mailings). Many churches say, in effect, "We lose $85 per year on each member. We are not willing to extend support to anyone, so you need to pay us at least that amount to be a voting member. We insist that you to be generous with us, but we cannot see our way to be generous with you. No one is entitled to be a burden on the community."

On the other hand, the congregation says that as long as a person or family is willing to pay this very minor amount the community is willing to grant them full and equal status in membership — no further contribution to our communal costs of running the church is required.

Either represents a strange standard for a religious community to hold forth; neither falls within the meaning of right relationship. Both approaches to setting forth a financial standard for membership are clearly unacceptable as a stewardship standard for members precisely because 98% of us can afford much more and more is required to maintain the community. "Community" carries the implication that all who choose to become members will support the joint enterprise. By "low-balling" our expectations, we undermine the covenant to be in community. We undermine the formation of generous attitudes that are at the foundation of spiritual health we seek in the first place.

Money, serious money, is the evidence of serious choices. The church "belongs" to those who take it seriously; so, serious financial commitment and membership are intertwined. "Serious money" is best defined not in absolute terms but rather as a percentage of income. It is the job of the leadership to articulate such a standard and then to support members in finding ways to embrace that standard as they embrace the community.

But how should we set a giving standard? If we set a required minimum commitment level of, say, $50/month for each member, we violate the serious notion that we are available to all without regard to income level. The very poor among us would be disenfranchised. At the same time, the wealthy individual who might make several times that much in a single hour is not meeting a giving standard worthy of his or her income.

Rather, consider using a percentage standard for setting stewardship expectations. For example, the leadership could ask everyone to donate at least one hour of their income each week to the church as a minimum.[4] Adoption of that standard by all members of congregations in my denomination would double the size of our church budgets. It is 2.5%.

When I talk about percentage giving in workshops, invariably someone will ask "Is that calculation made on gross, adjusted gross, or take-home?" Usually someone else wonders how we are to "enforce" percentage standards. "Are we," they ask loudly and disdainfully, "going to ask for a copy of their tax return?" These are natural questions, obvious questions, and, after some thought, irrelevant questions.

Helping people understand their own stewardship standard as a percent of their income has four purposes: First, it provides a benchmark: while not an enforceable rule, it sets an approach to start people thinking about their values within community life. Second, it provides more opportunity for people at all income levels to ask for acknowledgment of generous behavior even though their

---

4 It is easy to calculate: Most people know their annual income. Drop three zeroes and divide the remainder by two.

dollars are not as bountiful. It also provides an opportunity for the congregation to recognize those who feel they are generous (even while not offering dollar denominated evidence), and to express gratitude to them. Finally it provides some (somewhat skewed) data for the Finance Committee when looking to the future.

It's not an audit. No one will be quizzing respondents or challenging the answers. The worst case is that someone overstates their percentage contribution because they want to feel what it is like to be treated as a generous donor. *As a matter of faith, I think most parishioners will find a way to embrace a 2%, 5%, or 7% standard that is more sacrificial than any fixed dollar standard we might all agree on.*

There is no way out of the reality that we only offer guidance to our members: clear, helpful guidance. We do not need rules with the stiffness of an audit standard. We give away the hard dollar standard we can audit in favor of a malleable privately applied standard. Acceptance and interpretation of our guidance rests solely with each person and is part of their own struggle with commitment to community life. It is part of the individual's spiritual journey.

Monthly Contribution Commitments

Focus on the monthly amount with members. Train members to consider their relationship to the community as one that is continuous through time. We want to match the commitment of support to our member's income cycle. Because mortgage, credit card, and utility payments are on a monthly cycle, and because most of us receive income either monthly or semi-monthly we all define our financial lives within that temporal structure. Monthly finance is the context within which we most readily and accurately understand how much we can afford to give to others. Focus on the amount that members receive routinely each month and ask for a percentage of that amount.

> *"Joe and I want to move from 2% to a 3% sustaining member level over the next two years. We can't do it all at once; but we'll do half this year. You've been generously contributing a little more than 1% of your income each month. Could you join us in our long term goal and go to 1.5% a month at this time?"*

Most churches print stewardship cards on which members formalize their monthly commitment level. (See sample in Appendix 7) Ask members how much they prefer to pay monthly and which month they would like to start. Do not refer to an annual amount on the card. Most people do not consider their mortgage or their car payment in annual terms; do not ask people to think about the church in annual terms either. Ask them to think of it as a reasonable portion of their paycheck. Only the Finance Committee needs to use a calculator.[5]

Collecting the Monthly Commitment

The financial world is changing. Use flexible approaches to accepting payments. Some churches use on-line banking services to collect the stewardship commitment on a monthly routine. Most banks charge modestly for fund transfers in which case the church pays the fee. Such bank transfers do not require that the member pay any other bills in this manner; they simply authorize a monthly deduction from their checking or saving account to transfer to the church account. In such cases provide forms during the commitment drive to have funds automatically transferred from the member account on a particular date each month. (There are web based services that are even cheaper than most banks; see http://vancoservices.com for example.) These services are inexpensive and allowing members to set up automatic transfers means the monthly cash flow is vastly improved and full payment is more likely.

Some churches receive donations on credit cards. This costs the church in charges by the credit card company. It's okay to pay the credit card company — after all the church does not have to chase down the money. While most of us probably find putting our stewardship payment on a credit card a distasteful thought, it is not immoral. It can be an option.

Where I live we are allowed to use United Way to contribute to any not-for-profit organization, including churches. This is attractive for many people since payroll deduction is automatic and painless. People will increase their commitment level substantially if it is made less painful. However, the United Way organization withholds about 15% for administrative costs; but, at least it is part of the individual's tax deductible gift, unlike credit card interest.

Some church Treasurers have avoided these approaches, looking at their cost and seeing a loss. They offer advantages, however, in the certainty and regularity of the gift, in the substantial reduction in accounting workload, in getting funds deposited more quickly and in the possibility that the size of gifts will increase. There are costs of "business as usual" too – the reduction factor one must include in the annual budget when using only traditional collection methods, the cost in waiting for people to get around to paying stewardship commitments, and the

---

5 Note that the adoption of monthly pledging does not imply that the church needs to have a monthly budget. The church financial cycle is annual; the family financial cycle is monthly. The two are unrelated.

cost of tracking them down when they don't. So, look at all the costs as well as all the benefits of each possible method of collecting the monthly stewardship payments.

This chapter is important.[6] What follows is, I hope, a summary of what you encountered in this chapter, embellished by further observations:

1) Generous giving is a learned behavior pattern. The most effective means of teaching and learning any behavior is by modeling — in our case calling attention to those influential people who exhibit generosity, expecting others to follow the pattern, and rewarding them when they do so.

2) The decision about who is to make the solicitation for a gift is as important as the act of solicitation.

3) Never send an ungenerous giver to ask for a generous gift.

4) People give to causes they care about that address needs important to them.

5) Generosity increases when donors feel they are supporting higher values rather than lesser ones.

6) People feel inspired to support successes and the growth of successes, not to make up for failures or to maintain the status quo.

7) Generosity increases over time as our gifts are shown to advance our own social and religious values, and as we are acknowledged and affirmed for our specific efforts.

8) Persons soliciting gifts will be more effective when they know how much was given in the past, and have a specific gift target for this ask.

9) Donors do not give to support congregational budgets. They give to support commanding visions and well-articulated programs with realistic opportunities for achieving them.

10) People enjoy working on stewardship campaigns where they have confidence in the leadership and like the people they work with.

---

6 Many of the ideas put forth are not new, but need constant repeating. I am indebted to Rev. Ralph Mero for helping me crystallize my thinking in this area.

THREE STORIES

Story 1

Calvin Hobbes had recently been elected Chair of the Board of Trustees at a large church in suburban Cedar Falls. He was a professional mediator and labor dispute negotiator. He had spent the last 20 years dealing with group dynamics and settling conflicts. Everyone thought he would make a good congregational president.

He was concerned that his church lacked a coherent vision of its mission however. It was a comfortable place to worship, and the people who attended were warm and engaging. He was happy to have found the church when settling here after the bar exam. What was troubling however, was the comfortable, complacent routine of the congregation. Meanwhile, the roof was deteriorating and the religious education wing needed lots of attention, possibly even expansion. There was no thought being given to how the church might be able to do more in the community. The community service component of the budget was less than 3% of the total, including denominational requirements.

Calvin met with his minister one day to share these concerns, carefully guiding the discussion away from blaming anyone for the situation. Calvin knew it was a failure of the community, the entire leadership group, not specific individuals.

"We need to move the congregation into a new sense of itself over the next few years. The expansion of the university campus and the new high tech employment center means there will be new people in the area looking for a place to worship and serve. I'd like our congregation to be the place they choose."

"I've been feeling that way too," said Rev. Thom Katz. "Yet, I have been unable to stir up planning for a future you and I see so clearly. I'm interested in hearing your ideas. More importantly, I'd like to figure out how to launch a meaningful planning process."

"First, it's clear we need to have everyone involved," muttered Call, "even the goofballs. And, with everyone engaged there will need to be some structure to guide the congregation's discussion. We don't want to end up with a lot of individual ideas that don't have a coherent relationship to each other –or are so bland they sit there like a Jell-O salad, don't offer anything to sink your teeth into.

"We've got a damn fine group of trustees right now," Calvin continued. "I think we need to start by getting their ideas. Let's go on a retreat and ask them what they see as most important, things the congregation should be attending to that we're not."

"Yes, Cal," Rev. Katz broke in. "The trustees we have now are the best we've had in years, but we need to talk to a larger leadership group. I don't think the trustees alone can launch a successful visioning effort. There is a larger group; it's an informal group. They are the opinion leaders in our congregation however, the glue that holds us together."

"OK, but how do we figure out specifically who they are?" asked Calvin.

"It seems to me we should look at our list of members and think about who serves the congregation most heavily. I bet you and I can list them out in a few minutes. They constitute, at most, 20% of the members. Starting with our membership directory, let's give folks a point for serving on a committee sometime during the last three years, two if they were in charge. Also, other kinds of service should get points, like teaching in the religious education program, or helping consistently on Sunday mornings, even participating in the affiliational groups. People get points for each major, time-consuming effort – especially those most visible to others."

They went through the exercise to see where it would lead them. They could see that the point totals were obviously skewed around a relatively small group of members. Then, they also looked at the giving records of the past three years. They added two heavy contributors who were not already on the list of leaders, and one retired woman who was no longer able to give much of either her time or money, but who was respected by everyone as one of the founding members of the congregation. Their process was not science, simply instinct. When done they had 37 of the 243 members listed.

"I know there are others who have also been in the congregation for years. They talk a lot at congregational meetings," Rev. Katz continued, "but they don't ever seem to step up to the plate and give much, in any sense other than talk. We will hear from them eventually; and, we'll all listen. But, I don't think we need to solicit their opinions at this point."

"You're right," said Cal. "After all is said and done, the individuals we have already listed are vital to this congregation's health. What that group wants, the others will want too – or pretty much go along with. Yet, if that group doesn't get behind something, it won't happen."

Looking at the list they decided to have a series of small informal dinners at Cal's house over the course of the next three months. Dividing the list into smaller conversational-sized groupings, they saw they would need to hold six or seven such dinners, with a few extra spouses and partners included.

Rev. Katz said, "I want to be sure we have one of the current trustees at each dinner. And, while I do not need to be at all of them, I need to attend at least three so that I have an opportunity to listen to more than a single small group."

And so, they held the conversations. The key but unannounced focus was to ask at some point in the evening, "What do you see as missing that you would like to see our congregation doing three or four years from now? Don't worry about cost at all – just let your thoughts come as they will. How can we be a better church?"

After the series of conversations they had quite a list of ideas – but not a coherent vision or plan. They then scheduled a retreat with the Board, and let it be known that the Board would be talking about the possibility of launching a congregation-wide visioning process.

At the retreat Cal explained that they had each attended a dinner at his place during the last few months. In the course of those conversations, they would recall, there had been discussions about things that some people in the congregation felt needed improving. He handed out a list of the identified unfulfilled needs to be addressed. The group talked about the items individually for a couple of hours. There were differences of opinion expressed about their relative merit. New ideas were offered too.

Finally the Rev. Katz said, "I see three general themes being discussed here: First, people have expressed concerns about what happens on Sunday morning. We can broaden that notion a bit and refer to it as the quality of the spiritual journey. People seem to want the very best religious education for their children, and also want to engage in their own deepening awareness. There are several items that relate to the quality of the Sunday experience, but also an apparent desire for expansion of our adult enrichment programs.

"Second, there is a call for our congregation to more deeply impact on the larger world. This group thinks we are not engaged as strongly as we might be in social justice, environmental, and other concerns of that sort.

"Finally, and I am not quite sure how to label this, there are concerns expressed about the health of our relationships within the congregation. I see some ideas here that suggest that people want to assure there are strong personal connections, not only for themselves but also for all the newcomers who visit on Sundays. I see some suggestions here that I guess I would label as a call for strong, healthy interpersonal connections, including pastoral support.

"We could sit here and debate these items individually, but that doesn't address the more general concerns. I think those general ideas provide the format for a larger discussion of where the congregation wants to go."

He concluded by saying, "It's time to bring this discussion to the entire congregation. I suggest we call a day long planning session for all those who want to come. We could organize people into interest groups around the three areas I just identified. Then, we can use the specific list we already have simply to seed the conversation for each group. They are all worth talking about further by others. Let's have the congregation evaluate the individual ideas, add others, and put them all into a more coherent plan."

The others agreed that this breakdown was a pretty good way of sorting out the list. They would ask the members to pick one of the areas of most interest and form a working group for the day to think about that area of church life. They further determined that they would try to focus the congregational planning on a time five years into the future. And, they would encourage the discussion to not dwell too much with fiscal concerns. The participants would be asked to consider that, while resources were not unlimited, a doubling was going to occur over the next five years. They could each plan on uses for up to half of this amount to launch their ideas. The Treasurer had already made such a calculation.

The day was very successful in drawing many people, engaging them in serious discussion, and ending up with reasonably good thinking about how the congregation needed to change. Of course, the "opinion leaders" were there and were each pleased to see the ideas they thought important were included in the discussion. Their positive support was critical.

Rev. Katz preached on each of the areas during the next few months, which helped launch initiatives for the committees to begin working on. And, the Board directed the Finance Committee to develop a five year Vision Budget that would move the congregation in the chosen direction. In so doing, the Board agreed upon only two fundamental parameters: 1) that membership would increase at the rate of 5%/year; 2) that average per family giving would increase by 10%/year.

Calvin Hobbes finished his term as President two years later. He reflected on what had made the planning process work better during his tenure. He decided that it had been important to set the leadership into its role. They had not been given any official status or power, but they had been asked to lead.

Second, the congregational discussion had been focused. It had been an open discussion – but it was also seeded with ideas that were important in the eyes of the leadership. This allowed for plenty of room for the congregation to massage the contributions of the opinion leaders, but also assured key ideas were present in the discussion without names attached to them.

Finally, the Board had recognized that no plan is done until the details are addressed. In each of the three areas the Finance Committee had met with other related committees and groups to get agreement on the timing of various initiatives. The discussion that ensued after the Finance Committee had developed the costs of a five year program projection had been realistic and the congregation had excitedly pursued the initiatives outlined there.

It was a plan that could work for the congregation.

Story 2

Rev. Bob Jones of Maple Valley Unitarian Church had grown increasingly concerned about what he understood as a sense of scarcity among his parishioners that was not substantiated by the vacations they took, the cars they drove, and the homes they lived in. Yet, the national economy was in bad shape and scarcity thinking hung around like a low grade infection, bringing anxiety and inability to recognize their truly abundant lives.

He called together two couples in his congregation as well as a retired doctor whose partner had died some years ago. He told them he wanted their guidance and help in facing a difficult task. They were selected because they had all demonstrated strong support of his ministry and had been generous over the years. (He knew they were *very* wealthy.)

They gathered one evening and he explained he had been thinking about what he saw as a failure of spiritual awakening. He lamented that the members of the congregation were not enthusiastic about the church's ministry. He expressed his dismay that only about one-fourth of the givers could be called generous within their means. Many others were moderately supportive, but well over half the members were not contributing much at all to the church. Yet, despite the low giving levels many members over the years had expressed repeatedly "We're doing pretty much all we can do; we're tapped out."

Everyone around the table shared similar concerns and went through the data on the 165 families and individual givers in the congregation:

5)   Only 21 of the 165 gave more than $150/month currently, totaling $61,000/year – more than one third of all giving in the church.

6)   Another 46 averaged about $100/month.

7)   Nearly 100 currently gave less than $85/month, averaging about $35.

They all expressed frustration over an inability to move the congregants to a heartfelt sense of mission. Rev. Bob went further, suggesting that a person's giving and their notion of the congregation's mission in the community and in the world seemed to be closely intertwined. Congregants would not engage seriously and enthusiastically in a planning process that would move the church into a wider ministry. Many complained that such exercises were a waste of time and effort because the plans did little more than sit on the shelf since the congregation "could not afford them".

Realistically, they all agreed. The planning effort they had gone through four years ago was too general, not focused, and there simply wasn't a sense of reality to it. It was destined to the same dusty fate. Rev. Jones suggested that congregants seem to feel there was never going to be much change in giving, so why bother planning for changes (which always cost more money)?

On the other hand, people did not want to increase their gifts to the church because there was little in the way of a vision for change. People were not inspired to increase the commitment without some motivating sense that their increased gifts would make a difference. The congregants had money; they simply were not motivated to contribute it to the church. The congregation was locked into a "Catch-22."

He explained that he wanted them to consider changing the basis for their own annual giving this next year. Rather than commitments of a fixed amount he asked if they would consider simply matching the increases of other congregants. He had some numbers and together they determined that they would be giving somewhat more, but it could have valuable consequences. They too were willing to give more if it might make a difference somehow. They talked further.

A little later the doctor suggested expansion of the idea: "Suppose," he said, "that for all those who currently average less than $75/month we agree to match the increased giving over the next year 3:1. That is, if a family in that group gives more than their current gift level over the next year we could promise to match all the increase three times over.

"Suppose further that for those with average giving between $75 and $150 each month we would match their increases the same way, but at $2 for each $1 of increase. Then finally, for everyone already over $150/month we can match any increase dollar for dollar.

"This approach could cost us a lot more," he asserted, "but only if all those folks at the lower end increase their giving – which is what we want. Further, those who are on very limited income, do not give much and cannot increase their giving, would still know that any increase they can afford will be very meaningful."

Enthusiasm was building. One of the others suggested that they consider matching increases each year for three years. This might induce ever higher giving levels into the parishioners' overall spending habits, and probably create a longer-lasting effect. She was a professor in the finance department at the business school. She got out her calculator.

With some agreed upon assumptions they could see that the total cost to them could be as much as $425,000 over the three years, or $28,000 for each of them every year, but likely no more. But if that happens stewardship gifts by the rest of the congregation will increase from a current level of about $165,000/year to over $350,000/year – more than doubling. With their matching gifts added in, the congregation could receive about $1.3 million rather than the $500,000 expected from current giving patterns. Of course, this would only be worthwhile if the congregation stayed at a higher level rather than drifting back to $165,000 after the matching incentive stopped. That was the question; they would only know the answer by going ahead.

They went ahead. The five of them set up a small charitable foundation which they agreed to equally fund. The charity would, in turn, pay the matching funds to the church. Rev. Jones announced to the congregation that a small private – and anonymous – foundation which was interested in the problem of instilling personal generosity had chosen their church to make a wonderful offer. (All true!) He described the experimental matching program.

One person in the congregation stood during the ensuing discussion and wondered if this wasn't crass manipulation – and "should not be done in a church of all places."

One of the trustees suggested they were all being manipulated every day – for example when he had decided to buy a bottle of wine with a pretty label rather than the more modest one he initially looked at. He asserted that rewards and punishments are the reality, the glue, of societal life. They need not be understood as exclusively negative in character. He pointed out that the offer being made was manipulation designed to bring out the best in each of them. In fact he proffered that he attended church specifically to be manipulated into being a better person. It could not be a bad thing. The members applauded and agreed to participate in the experimental program.

So, what happened? Membership increased by 50% because of the excitement that was so evident in joyful programs and attitudes. This was a positive but unexpected consequence of the initiative. The number of pledging families increased from 165 to 223 during the three years.

Rather than only 21 families giving more than $150/month, there were now 72; and only 37 family units were below $85/month. Average giving over the three years went from about $85/month to more than $200. All the new families understood the stewardship expectation; in practice their giving was quite high too even though it was not included in the matching program. Total stewardship income in the third year (without the matching funds) was more than $500,000 rather than the $350,000 expected, and three times the level of earlier years.[7]

More people felt they knew what it meant to be generous, and they kept doing it because they were part of a church community that was making the world a better place. They felt their own lives were better for it too.

---

7 Get out a pencil (with an eraser) and your own calculator. These are not wild, exaggerated expectations.

Since it was clear there was going to be an increasing budget, the congregation became alive to the opportunity of planning to increase their services. They spent the first of the three years in a serious effort at focusing on creating new programs both within the church and in service to the larger community.

A Community Minister was hired. The congregation became heavily involved in serving two local charities. They also decided to "adopt" a young African woman who wanted to come to the U.S. to study music.

The congregation hired a full time adult learning director who began creating lifespan learning programs for adults every evening during the week. There were also outstanding programs in the Sunday school, and there were adequate supplies – and cookies.

The congregation promised three troubled and at-risk teens in the youth group that they would help support them in attending college or community college. All they had to do was focus harder in high school and get admitted. The Community Minister worked with them too, bringing other supportive services to bear.

There was money available to help congregants attend important denominational meetings and trainings which brought more members into a deeper connection with the denomination and with the ministry of the congregation.

Some said it was a modern day miracle. Rev. Bob and the anonymous leaders knew it did not require divine intervention; it was an exercise of human will – a matter of breaking through habitual patterns of thought which lead to habitual self-defeating behaviors.

Story 3

Rev. Sue Ellerson raced to the gas station near her church. It was 2:30 in the morning. One of her congregants was hiding in the mini-mart however, having apparently been beaten again by her husband. This was a continuing saga in the Bronson household, a secret known by very few in up-scale St. James Church in the Woods. Her congregation was removed from such realities in so many ways – the income, educational, and social status differences seemed to wrap them in a protective cocoon while also shutting them off from the realization that others suffered, even among their friends.

She decided however that the reality needed to be shared with her Board of Trustees. She knew there were other situations in the congregation which defined the dark side of any community, including hers – alcoholism, abused children, and bankruptcy to name a few.

When she talked to her Board a month later, she related some of the stories that were part of the life of the congregation, stories that don't get told in nicer churches like theirs. The President of the Board wept as he explained that these stories brought forth his own memories of a favorite cousin who had been murdered by her husband a few years ago. The family had not been aware of the difficulties she had faced in her marriage. "I am so angry at myself for not helping," he said. "I was oblivious, and didn't do anything over all those years."

That evening the Board decided they would launch two new efforts in the congregation. First, they needed to train a cadre of laity who would engage in pastoral work; they needed more talent available simply to be present in members' lives in a way that would be conscious of the signals of distress. They decided to hire a well known psychologist in the community to help the minister design and offer a program of effective pastoral counseling.

Second, they decided that their highest priority in the upcoming budget year was to get the congregation involved in the social services of their community, particularly the shelters, halfway houses, and runaway teen programs – all of which had direct relevance to their membership as evidenced in Sue's stories. To do this they would ask the congregation to extend their efforts by calling a community minister into service with them. Such a service would increase the budget by another 10%. The Trustees agreed to push hard for that increase.

Three years later Rev. Ellerson reflected on the changes that had occurred in her congregation. There was a much higher interest throughout in being in service to each other. For example, they now had six members designated as pastoral chaplains. One of the chaplains was so excited about what he was doing that he had decided to end a first career, return to school, and study to become a full time adolescent and teen therapist.

A new part-time Associate Minister was developing strong connections between the congregation and some of the service agencies in the community. While he had focused initially on the issues evident within the congregation, that was changing. Now a group wanted to get involved in a literacy program serving a nearby immigrant community. There was another group involved in a work-release program with a nearby correctional facility.

Others had opened their lives to service too. There was a pool of drivers providing transportation for the elderly. There was an after school activities program with some of the teens helping care for the youngsters. And, the casserole brigade now had several members rather than the two who had done that work for so many years. Everywhere she turned there were members in support of others.

Rev. Ellerson talked about the changes over a beer one evening with her Associate Minister. "What happened here?" she asked. "Why did this congregation change over the last three years from ignoring the difficulties of others to being heavily in ministry to them?"

"First," explained Rev. Inquvist, "you got their attention by showing them that their own friends in the church have problems that they need to work on as a community. That's a huge step – simply getting their attention; and, by showing them things affecting them directly and viscerally they wanted to help. Everyone wants to help, but mostly on problems to which they feel connected."

"Second, you called me," he said jokingly.

"You're right," said Rev. Ellerson, "and it's not a joke. The church has had someone to focus our attention, so the initial efforts have been more successful. From those early successes you have shown the members that what they do matters; it makes a difference. And, by awakening that interest in making a difference, they want to reach out to serve other communities. They now recognize the importance of their service in bringing meaning to their lives."

After finishing their beers they went back to church for another meeting.

FUNDS

How many do we really need? . . . . Really?

A church is an entity. We report on such an entity when we prepare financial statements. Some church organizations create and report on many "funds". Separate reports on the general operating, capital, flower, organ, family retreat, needy family, and many other "funds" are sent to the Board (perhaps).[8] While there are serious interests which must be respected in earmarking the use of gifts to a purpose, it is not necessary to physically isolate the monies. That is the *reason* for accounting.

I have been in conversation with congregations with multiple bank accounts, each established in pursuit of having good control over particular gifts, or monies raised for a particular purpose. Every time a member of the congregation would give a special gift for some purpose, for example, or if the Board decided to "set aside" funds for some longer term purpose, this was understood to mean a new bank account. Sometimes various committees have separate bank accounts – perhaps because they had charged a fee and wanted to keep "their money" separate.

All these separate accounts were given the name "the X Fund" and reported on separately to the board, if at all. Most congregations, in truth, have at least an Operating Fund and a Building (or Capital) Fund. Historically it may have made sense to manage various pots of money this way. It may have been easier "way back when." It is not easier in the new millennium. We have good software which keeps track of transactions in a more complete chart of accounts. So, why would we still want to conduct our affairs as though we operate out of several shoe boxes? It is clumsy and confusing to create several different bank accounts for a church simply because someone believes some money needs to be protected and controlled. And in truth, the Board members at such churches will usually tell you they feel they have less control, not more. The church is a single entity; report on it in a single, consolidated format.

---

8 We are not referring to a bank account or brokerage account. It is possible for a church to operate with a single fund (have consolidated financial statements) which includes more than one bank account. In fact, it is unusual for a church with substantial amounts of money to keep it all in a checking account, even unwise. A good treasurer will assure that the church's spare cash is invested in higher interest bearing certificates of deposit, or even stocks and bonds if warranted.

Attractive Considerations of a Single Fund

1) **It is easier to understand the fiscal affairs of the church if they are consolidated.** It is easier to see all the support coming into one place. It is easier to keep track of how money is used as it flows out of one place, and it is easier to see that it is used as intended. It is easier both for those who are in responsible leadership roles and for members who simply want to stay informed.

2) **It is easier to manage the cash resources of the church if they are pooled.** If not, a church might have perpetual problems in meeting its obligations during the summer, while having a great deal of cash isolated in dedicated accounts.

   I don't understand an accounting scheme which values a set of fairly arbitrary financial distinctions ahead of the immediate responsibilities of salary or other bills. Let us be clear here: This is not a call for setting aside the intended uses of funds, such as might be recognized by a separate account. Rather, a church budget controls how money will be spent better than the existence of various "pots". The fundamental purpose of the budget is to control how much money is spent, for what, and when. The congregation holds the Board accountable for ensuring that both the income and expenses fit the budget. If the Board is doing its job, separate accounts are distracting and irrelevant.

3) **It is better financially to have a single large account because of reduced bank charges, or possibly increased interest income on account balances.** Many banks have more attractive arrangements for accounts with more than a $1,000 minimum balance. If committees have separate accounts, they may not meet that requirement

4) **It is easier for the congregation to understand and meet their priority needs with a single fund and a single annual stewardship drive.** Thus, the community is healthier and more trustful of itself as it achieves better balance in its vision. When there is a single vision and a single annual stewardship drive, separate funds are an oxymoron. When there is not, separate funds reinforce the apparent dispersion of interests.

5) **No obligation should be honored ahead of other obligations as a matter of routine policy.** "Funds" contribute to the delusion that such behavior by the congregation is permissible. For example, the mortgage

or loans a church has are fixed obligations. If the church does not have a successful "capital annual stewardship drive" the obligations must still be paid. They must be paid whether or not there is cash in the "capital fund". The same is true for the salaries of the staff or the bill for office supplies. All obligations have equal standing; it is unconscionable to not meet the financial obligations of the church while money is available in a separate "fund".

Despite all these good reasons for going to consolidated reporting, there may still be some lingering doubts. Some readers will be thinking "Yes, but … that's the way we've been doing it." When pressed, treasurers tell me "that's the way we've been doing it" because someone or some group fears a loss of control over the way money is spent. But the loss of control comes from having inadequate accounting records and unintelligible financial reports, not from merging the finances *per se*. Good reports make readily apparent how much each committee has received and spent. Good reports show precisely the total church mortgage, the amount paid already, and the amount due to be paid yet this year.

When church treasurers do not readily convey the information other leaders want to see, there is a desire to isolate the funds of interest and to ask for separate reports. That's the only way the untrained know to ask for the information and control they feel is needed. The job of the financial steward is to show a way to achieve better control through better and more complete information.

The Taxable Income Corporation

We are focusing on the notion that we have a single community entity and want to have the financial expression of that entity reflected in unified financial reports. There is a circumstance, however, in which a second entity needs to be recognized, created, and separated financially. If a church (or any non-profit organization for that matter) derives a significant amount of revenue from sales or rentals or in ways which look like any ordinary business, there needs to be a new tax-paying entity created for the unrelated and business-like activities. The danger in not doing so is that the IRS may declare the church a sham as a church and in reality a small business. If so church income is entirely taxable to the church, and gifts are no longer deductible by donors.

So, if you have a church which derives, say, more than 15% of its income in ways that do not have anything to do with the spiritual purposes of the church, see an attorney. Set up a Taxable Income Corporation which can then run the bookstore, rent the parking lots for park and ride during the week, rent the building, and manage all the other profitable and less religious activities for the church. This company will then file a tax return and pay taxes. The remaining income is donated to the church. The directors of the Corporation can be the trustees of the church. The administrator of the Corporation can be, and probably should be, a distinct appointment.

Endowment Funds

An endowment fund is a special creature which is established with a separate standard of prudence: It is to last perpetually and provide continuous support for some activity. For example, when a donor gives stock and bonds to the church and asks that the income from the portfolio be used to bring aesthetic enhancement to the worship service, the gift has a decidedly different character than a regular monthly payment. While the gift has a purpose of general church support which might also be found in the ongoing budget, it also has a special requirement of stewardship of the principal in perpetuity. *Because it has a different standard of prudence associated with it, it must be isolated* in a separate fund. When understood from this perspective, it is fairly easy to see why an endowment fund is isolated.

On the other hand, a gift designated to a particular purpose, such as the purchase of a pipe organ, relates to an objective for spending. The gift can be reserved within the general church accounts until the money is used for its designated purpose in the future. The reserves may exist for several years, but the money is not subject to a standard of perpetual existence. The gifts given for an eventual spending need are given for a purpose which does not require a more rigorous standard of prudence or care. Therefore, the establishment of a separate Organ Fund or Building Fund is unnecessary, burdensome, and inappropriate.

Many churches set up an endowment fund even if the fund has no money in it. The existence of the fund brings a focus to the membership for particular enduring gifts the community might want to make. It need not be complicated. The following points should be integrated into the design of the endowment fund.

1) Establishing an endowment fund need not involve the entire community. A simple *Statement of Governance and Processes* can be adopted by the board. (See sample in Appendix 9.) It is appropriate for the endowment to be separately governed; but the church trustees can set up the endowment with that objective in mind.

2) Establishing the programs or objectives of the endowment fund, on the other hand, must involve the entire community. Every time an enduring program is debated and identified as worthy of the endowment fund, it must be done in a process that involves the entire community, rather than

allowing a small sub-group or individual to determine the priorities of the community's enduring gifts program.

3) Every endowment fund must have specific, identifiable program objectives which benefactors can focus on. For example, a congregation might decide that it wants a campus ministry at the nearby community college. It is determined by the Finance Committee that such a program will cost at least $20,000 each year and that an endowment fund of $250,000 could generate $12,500 annually dedicated to this purpose. The congregation adopts an enduring gifts objective of raising $250,000 by the year 2012. Every subsequent report on the endowment fund includes that enduring gift objective as well as the amount actually collected.

Without naming specific enduring programs in the endowment fund, the congregation is engaged in fantasy — the implication is that there will be enduring gifts for support of basic programs. "Then we'll be on Easy Street. We won't be short on the budget anymore." This is a strange pattern of thought. It should be fairly evident that the church which has perennial problems with its budget is hardly going to obtain huge enduring gifts so that future members can commit to even smaller amounts than are required to support the current programs.

Most enduring gifts are not given so that the congregation can be relieved of the need to support itself. They are given almost always because the benefactor wants to empower some very special activity. Thus, it is more difficult to attract enduring gifts when no attractive ideas for the use of such gifts are offered.

4) The *Statement* must establish that the endowment fund will be isolated from the regular funds of the church. It should be stipulated that there will be no borrowing of principal from the endowment. What benefactors want to know above all else when they make such gifts is that the gift will endure through any hard times the church may encounter. Thus, the church must be precluded from access to the *corpus* of the gift.

5) The *Statement* must define income. My preference is to name a percentage of the average (quarterly or monthly) fund size over the prior three years and define that as income. The standard can be either fixed or variable as in the following two examples: a) "fixed at 5%", or b) "Equal to the 10 year Treasury Bond rate on each December 31". Defining income in this way

will enable the fund to produce income every year, whatever the cycle of the investments produces. For the long term, this is a conservative and preferable way of determining income because it allows for more broadly diversified investments, including those which do not yield current interest or dividends. It is also helpful to state clearly that all income will be reinvested and not spent until some threshold is passed — for example, "No income shall be used to support enduring projects until at least 75% of the required principal is obtained."

6) Finally the *Statement* must define who is responsible for oversight of the endowment funds and how the eventual income will be disbursed.

I suggest appointing rather than electing endowment fund directors. A church community is a relatively small and homogenous collection of values. Separate elections create an impression that there are complex, diverse interests that need to be accounted for. More frequently the problem is one of assuring there is a coordinated effort by the entire community in pursuit its multi-year plans. The enduring nature of endowment gifts requires the development of bylaws to protect the intentions of benefactors; that is different, however, from programmatic fracturing that can result too easily from endowment directors who believe they are doing their job only when they are questioning the intentions of the board leadership, or mistakenly thinking that the only way to serve the congregation is by creating a unique program.

An endowment committee might consist of five members. One should be the pastor or minister, or their appointee. I suggest that this appointment, if there is one, be done annually and that there be no limitation on the time served. Two members can be appointed from among the board members. These members will incur a natural turnover based upon the turnover of board membership. Finally, the board should appoint two people from among the membership at large. While I am not a fan of term limits, I understand that many are. If there are to be limitations on the service of the at-large members they should be for a single term which is fairly long, due to the very specialized knowledge which develops on an endowment committee.

COMPENSATION MANAGEMENT

Employee costs comprise two-thirds or more of a standard church budget. This alone makes it important for financial leaders to understand how the numbers are arrived at, and why this person is paid such and such while another costs much more. Beyond that however, all church leaders have an interest in the employment environment they help create for their staff. Costs are a big factor in the environment, but there are others too. Most churches are pretty lax in thinking about personnel policy and practices. But, churches as employers have a responsibility to be rigorous in exploring the underlying values, subsequent design, and the implementation practices of employee relations. We expect this Monday through Friday when we go to work; we owe the same to our staff.

Employer Philosophy

Staff compensation decisions are grounded in values. The values are either chosen and articulated or they are implied – meaning they are unarticulated, chosen by default, and frequently less noble. Why not be clear in choosing? Isn't life in a church community foremost about clarifying the values we wish to live by, then working deliberately to integrate them into our decision-making?

Every congregation with staff should develop and adopt a statement of employment philosophy. This does not mean making pie-in-the-sky statements simply because they sound good; rather, the statement might simply say that the church intends to pay according to the prevailing wage structure in the area or according to some alternate standard, that certain benefits will be available, that every staff person knows where to turn for supervision and for redress of grievances, whether membership in the congregation – or one's religious beliefs – will preclude employment. There are many issues to address and many ways to address them. Every congregation will handle the issues differently. No one can dictate a Statement of Employment Philosophy to your congregation. If your congregation needs a sample to start the discussion however, see Appendix 2.

Distinguishing Employment Types

There are several different ways in which churches hire people, full-time vs. part-time being an obvious distinction.[9] The different employment relationships can, if you choose, effect the way you apply pay and benefit standards. We sometimes think that all employees "really should" be treated the same, and in that righteous stand can spend hours discussing how to dole out holiday leave pay, for example, to those who provide child care as needed for evening meetings I outline five employment categories here, and will use them later to make distinctions about compensation and benefits.

Ministers are in a special category of their own. The prevailing doctrine, in most protestant denominations at least and which I have no interest in disputing, is that the nature of the Call to a congregation sets them apart from the standard employer/employee relationship. They usually operate within an agreed Letter of Understanding which is developed at the time they first come to the congregation. (There are surely many other names for the agreement.) The Letter of Understanding is not a contract, although most attorneys think it "looks like a duck, quacks like a duck ..." The Letter of Understanding frequently is not written with great precision, but offers general guidelines and hopes for both the minister and the congregation. That too is by choice and mutually satisfactory.

I believe most would agree that the ministerial Letter of Understanding is the foundation for the ministerial relationship. Other policies of the board do not supersede the Letter. Nonetheless, where other personnel policies do not contradict the letter they can be understood to amplify it.

Salaried employees are those whose rate of pay is determined on an annual basis. It may be broken into monthly or weekly increments for payment purposes, but it is established as an annual amount. Such employees do not have an hourly rate and are usually not asked to keep track of specific hours worked. The implication of a salaried job in a church is that the responsibilities are less routine, are more likely to have programmatic or professional work objectives, and less likely to be supervised as to specific tasks. Salaried employees are more likely to be required to interact with members (such as attending committee meetings) to fulfill the requirements of the job. They are more likely to work at home, perhaps regularly.

The danger for those in salaried positions, particularly when they are part-time, is that the congregation may ask more of them than can be accomplished in the hours paid for. Even though salaried employees are not keeping track of specific

---

9 I am not an attorney. I am not stating anything I know to be contrary to the law, but what I say may brush up against legal prohibitions. What I say in this chapter reflects only my own simple understandings. If you think you need to consult an attorney on personnel issues, you probably should.

hours worked, "full time" suggests that the job usually can be accomplished in about 40 hours each week; one-half time means the responsibilities should be manageable in about 20 hours a week.

A heuristic guide for thinking about how much time salaried employees might work is to think of a workweek as consisting of "units" of time, not hours. A "unit" is a morning, an afternoon, an evening. A standard church workweek consists of 12 units, which for most of us would be analogous to a 40 hour week with an additional expectation of putting in a couple of evenings or a Saturday morning to do our job the way we want to. Similarly, a quarter-time person should work three units most weeks – a full day plus an evening meeting perhaps, or Sunday morning.

Regular Hourly employees are paid by the hour and have an established work schedule. There may be flexibility in the schedule, but it is usually set around particular hours. Regular hourly employees work on site, as a rule. The work performed is more likely to be routine or consist of repetitive tasks. It is less likely to involve in depth interaction with members of the congregation or attending committee meetings.

All employees paid on a quarter-time basis or more probably fall into either the salaried or regular hourly category. It is easily possible for a regular hourly employee to work less than quarter-time. It is less likely that salaried responsibilities would require less than quarter-time.

Casual or Intermittent employees are paid on an hourly basis but have no routine schedule. If there is a routine time for performing the duties, there is frequently a pool of people who share the work, although one of them might be the leader. They usually agree among themselves on a work schedule, at the convenience of the members of the group. Thus, any individual employee may work very sporadically or only occasionally. A common example of such employees in my own experience is the small group who prepare coffee on Sunday mornings. The congregation wants coffee every Sunday at coffee hour, and someone to clean up; but, they are not concerned with who is there in particular. There may be other examples that come to mind from your experience.

Finally, some employment relationships are **contractual**. There are a number of IRS guidelines useful in determining whether a particular employee can be considered contractual. The default is that one is not a contractor unless it can be clearly established. A contract employee, for example, usually works their own hours, is given broad direction but not directly supervised, provides their own tools or materials, probably has other customers, and probably has a professional designation or business license. The guidelines are frequently overlooked in church employment, and the consequences can be difficult.

These employment categories are not hard and fast and you may not use them all, or you may modify the definitions. I find them serviceable in thinking about employment issues.

Relating Compensation to Employment Type

Clearly, those who are on a salary, and not keeping track of individual hours, do not get overtime pay. Just as clearly however, they get paid holidays and paid vacations which we will cover in greater detail later.

Regular hourly employees get overtime pay or compensatory time when they work more than forty hours in a week, sometimes they are paid overtime for any hours beyond their standard schedule. Overtime pay is higher than the standard hourly rate, frequently time-and-a-half. The employer has more discretion in setting the hours to fit the workload with hourly employees however, and when the workload is light the hours can be cut back resulting in savings. Such employees frequently do not get paid holiday and paid vacation time although an employer is not precluded from offering them.

Congregations sometimes employ someone on a "salaried" basis to avoid paying overtime, paying one-quarter time salary, and expecting routinely 12 – 15 hours each week. The duties evolve to a situation in which the expectations of the job cannot possibly be met in the time being paid for. Or, the congregation "gives" the salaried individual two months of unpaid vacation in the summer.

These are both too common examples of niggardly practices by churches in my opinion. If a workload dissipates in the summer months, the employee is not needed. The congregation saves money by reducing the paid hours. The employee is hourly, and should be receiving overtime while working the rest of the year. If the congregation understands a particular set of duties as requiring a salaried employee, the congregation should also agree to a paid vacation plan. If the paid vacation is to be two months long, fine. That is a choice. If the compensation is not increased in the annual budget, it will give the congregation a realistic assessment (from the employee's perspective) of what the true monthly salary is on a year around basis.

Casual and Intermittent employees do not get overtime, nor paid vacations, nor holidays. By the nature of the employment with its sometimes occasional work patterns varying greatly from one person to the next (think of the coffee crew) it seems tortuous, pretentious, and silly when churches struggle to establish levels of vacation or holiday pay for intermittent and casual employees, to me at least. Further, unlike salaried or regular hourly employees there is usually one fixed hourly rate which all casual and intermittent employees in a particular job get, and it is unaffected by longevity or merit increases.

Holidays

Every congregation should clearly specify holidays which it will pay for employees who qualify. Usually there are eight or ten paid holidays during the year, but it is up to you to specify which will be recognized. Because of the irregular nature of the church workweek, it can be confusing as to how to apply the holiday benefit. Let's start by understanding that nearly every regular holiday falls one per week. If employees birthdays are a recognized holiday it is quite possible to have two holidays in a week, but that is an easily handled exception. If there is a week with a holiday, every qualifying staff member should get one-fifth of their normal hours as holiday pay during that week. Thus, whether or not the holiday falls on a normal workday for a particular employee, s/he gets some holiday pay.

Suppose, for example, a regular hourly employee works half-time, normally Sunday morning plus at least all day on Thursday and Friday. If a holiday falls on Tuesday this employee should not be denied recognition of it. Rather, the employee gets one-fifth of the normal 20 hours, or four hours, of holiday time during that week. The person might agree to not come in until noon on Thursday of that week. Or, the person might work the normal schedule and get four hours of extra paid time that week. Similarly, if a holiday falls on Friday that individual should not get their workweek reduced by a full day. The workweek can be rearranged so that they do not come to the office on Friday; but, they still work 16 hours during the week, reducing the normal workweek by four hours for the holiday.

Annual Leave and Sick Leave

Let's begin by distinguishing the mechanics of these types of leave. Annual leave is planned for ahead of time jointly by the employee and the employer in such a way as to be least disruptive to the work flow. And, employees, in general, use annual leave for several days at a time; they return to work invigorated and happy. Ideally we would like all leave taken to be annual leave if it met those conditions.

Annual leave is good for employees and good for the organization. We want employees to use it. We should make an effort, then, to not create incentives for saving it. We should see that annual leave gets used regularly and the balance is near zero occasionally.

Sick leave is disruptive. When it is needed there is no way around it. An employee will call in one morning and explain they face a medical issue and will not be at work as expected. Tough. Sick leave will be granted immediately without further thought. We want employees to have sick leave available as a benefit. We would rather that they never have to use it. We want the incentive to be that employees would not want to use sick leave unless it is necessary. We want them try to save sick leave for the future.

Organizations which tell employees that their annual leave balance will be cashed out when they terminate but their sick leave balance will be lost seem to have it backwards. They ask employees, in effect, to always call in sick when they feel like taking a day off, but get the annual leave balance as high as possible rather than take a vacation. These incentives are not good for the organization and not good for the employee.

My own preference is to create a single leave plan called "personal leave". It is always available either for sick leave or annual leave purposes. At the end of each fiscal year any remaining personal leave balance not used that year is divided on some basis between a "permanent account" and a "temporary account".[10] The temporary account balance must be used in the following year or it will be lost, never cashed out. The permanent account balance can build up until the employee terminates, or it can be used – it is always available.

The permanent account will be cashed out at the current wage rate when the employee terminates however. This creates a huge incentive for the employee to build up a long term emergency leave account to have in the event of a major illness. But, any use of leave which is not arranged at least one week ahead of time is always charged first to the permanent account balance if there is one. Thus, to the maximum extent possible the employee incentive is to plan leave and get it approved well ahead of time so that it is not charged to the permanent account.

Benefits and Retirement

The most common benefits, other than leave policies, are various types of insurance and a pension or retirement plan. Sometimes only those who are full time employees get benefits (except qualified retirement plans in the U.S. usually *must include* those who are half-time or more). Usually however, any benefits available to full time staff are also available to other salaried or regular hourly employees who are half-time or more.

Sometimes an employer can simply provide access to a group insurance plan; it is a benefit to offer even if the employer doesn't contribute toward the cost. Dental, vision, life, and long term disability insurance plans are common examples which will be made available but frequently paid for entirely by the employees in the church setting.

Health insurance is far and away the highest cost benefit for U.S. employers – if they pay for it entirely, which fewer and fewer do. Further, it is probably the most used benefit in its frequency of need. Rather than going into a diatribe on

---

10 For example, the employer might allow each employee to transfer unused hours up to the number of hours in the employee's normal weekly schedule to the permanent account. Any remaining hours go into the temporary account.

the health system in this country and how we pay for it, let's simply agree that it is prohibitively expensive for the people we hire in churches to get health care without insurance or other assistance. So the church must help.

The cost of health insurance for the employer can be equal for every employee – fixed at, say, 80% of the premium. More likely the cost will vary with the time worked. One example would be for the church to offer to pay the same percentage as time worked in a normal week, up to a maximum of 80%. Thus, the church would pay half the premium for half-time staff and so on. This support would probably be applied only to those one-quarter time or more.

The more a church does to support employees in obtaining health insurance and other benefits the more devoted the employees will be. There are a small number of well-known companies which go to great lengths to assure that workers have health insurance. Starbucks, for example, pays fully for health insurance for those who are one-half time or more. Think of the difference between walking into a Starbucks store and a Walmart. Starbucks spends more on its employees, a lot more; no question. As employers, congregations need to determine whether the extra costs of benefits translate into better staff.

Compensation

Churches pay notoriously low salaries. Saying so means we have a compensation standard, of course, by which we make this judgment. Most church leaders would agree that the staff are not getting wealthy, and are probably not paid as much as they could be elsewhere. But, this is only a feeling for most of us – articulated occasionally and never documented. This huge proportion of our budget is usually unexamined and unexplained.

Review the existing staff position descriptions. Every job starts with a job title, and then is amplified with statements of responsibilities and expectations. A good job description will also indicate what the employee should bring to the job in the way of knowledge, experience, skills and abilities. Denominational resources are available to assist the personnel committee – refer to them. You do not have to follow their suggestions, but even a curmudgeonly lay person should look at the suggestions of church professionals to see whether they might be helpful.

Part of the job description involves a determination whether the job will be compensated on an hourly or salary basis. And of course, every complete job description has an associated pay range — an identified entry level and top level. Again, there are suggested salary ranges available from denominational sources.[11] If you are not comfortable with the suggestions, do not understand them, or think you can do better — do your own salary survey and make your own decision about

---

11 Or, look at the Compensation Handbook for Church Staff. This is a multi-denominational salary and compensation survey which is updated annually. Find it at http://store.churchlawtodaystore.com

what a staff person's job entails and what you will pay for that job. If your decisions comply with the employment philosophy you have articulated, and if you can hire the type of people your congregation deserves, your established salary and benefits structure exemplifies your own good decisions.

The congregation still needs to determine how much to pay within the established pay range. It is not enough to simply pick any number in the range and say, in effect, "We're OK. We're in there." We need to make it clear to the staff, the board, and the congregation why it is that one person is barely in their range while another is 30% of the way through it.

One common factor in marking progress through the pay range is longevity. Some argue against longevity in setting a pay level. They say, "Why should we increase pay simply because someone is keeping their seat warm?" This strikes me as a cynical attitude toward your staff. Sure, a small minority of people do not grow with the job. Most church employees work hard to improve their performance however. Longevity increases recognize improvement which is not noticeable in the standard employee evaluation process.[12] An employee gains responsibility and authority over time and is more effective working within the unique culture of a congregation. We recognizer this increasing capability with longevity increases.

As an example, let's establish the bottom of each range as the "base pay". Then, create eight steps to cover the range, each step being 12.5% further along selected range. More steps may lead to pay adjustments that are too miniscule to be noticed by the employee.

These longevity increases should go on for a number of years, but not necessarily every year and not forever. Further, I suggest not having longevity alone take anyone beyond half way through their range. The higher end of the range is attained only through other formally assessed factors discussed below. As an example, consider the following scale:

First Year	base
First Anniversary	1st step
Second	2nd step
Third	3rd step
Fifth	4th step (top for longevity)

This means the standard practice is for everyone to start at the bottom of their range and after five years everyone gets a rate at least 50% of the way through the range for their job, whatever the range is at that time.

---

12 3. In truth, most churches don't have an employee evaluation process that can be trusted. Recognizing longevity is a good proxy for some of the evaluative effort we fail at. I am not arguing this point as "either/or". Both are useful.

It is important to understand that it is not written in stone that everyone must start out at the bottom of the pay range however. A person with twenty years experience building a career in other congregations would no doubt bristle at the suggestion that he or she *must start at the bottom* in accepting a position with your congregation, just as though you were bringing on someone with no experience at all. When we hire a minister or a religious education director, for example, we might agree to give recognition to previous experience because it is worth something. We could negotiate in the hiring process for someone with four years of excellent previous experience to start as though they have three years with our congregation. Our standard practice in doing so might be for the new person to thereafter simply follow the rest of the pattern, two years later going from third step to fourth step based on longevity.

A good pay system will also recognize the extra training and education that one of our staff has pursued. It is sometimes significant enough to be rewarded. Suppose our youth minister completes a Master's degree in adolescent psychology. This is directly relevant to her current job and career choice. It establishes additional professional credentials. We should probably deal with it in the compensation arena or face possibly losing this key person. Our pay policy might say that any salaried employee can be considered for an additional step increment within the range for each year of professional career development training.   ·

Finally, we need a system to establish work goals, and evaluate how they are accomplished. A good pay system has built in capacity to reward superior performance. We might have annual superior performance increments as high as two steps of the range. This does not mean that one of our staff could necessarily exceed the top of the range – that too is a matter for thoughtful consideration in the employment philosophy and implementation policies.

The entire discussion to this point has been about how to establish a particular amount that we should pay a particular employee within their range. Suppose that, as so many churches find, when the personnel committee completes all the initial work of defining jobs and setting pay ranges they find great discrepancies between what we are doing now and what we say we want to do. Suppose further that the discrepancies range from very small for some positions to very large, but in total will cost more than we can possibly accomplish immediately.

What is required is that the congregation (not just the board) needs to decide upon a multi-year goal which will take it to employment practices compatible with the adopted employment philosophy. The job of the personnel committee is then to determine how to approach annual increments to attain the goal. Should every staff person receive some adjustment every year? Should we concentrate most heavily initially on those who are furthest behind? Should we start with just salary adjustments, or just the health insurance implementation? Each congregation must come to its own resolution.

I have summarized this chapter's main thoughts in spreadsheet format for two positions in the church, a minister and a part-time office administrator. You might want to develop similar documentation as part of your budget process to capture the historical record of decisions for each staff person. (See Appendix 11)

THE CHART OF ACCOUNTS

The key to getting useful information later.

The purpose of the chart of accounts is to summarize financial data. A church organization has literally hundreds or thousands of separate financial transactions occurring every year. These need to be sensibly summarized. Hence, the chart of accounts.

The chart of accounts gives detail to all the major categories of the balance sheet: assets, liabilities, reserves, accumulated surplus, and revenues and expenses.[13] There are many accounts and sub-accounts in each of these six areas because it is not possible to talk clearly about the financial affairs of the church without knowing more detail on each.

There is always a tugging in two directions in establishing that further detail. We want information we can retrieve in the most minute detail; most of the time we also want the details summarized in a way which is useful. There is no correct and timeless answer to this duality. Consequently, it is important to review the various account categories periodically and to add, diminish, or re-sort them.

Usually one needs to reduce the number of accounts. My rule of thumb is that if there are very few separate transactions being recorded in a particular account each year, it isn't doing much work for you. (For example, why would one have "insurance" as a line item with one premium payment each year? When was the last time someone had a question about the insurance premium?) Alternatively, if no one has asked for a particular piece of financial information or used it in some decision in the last three years, it is suspect as to its necessity as a separate account. Computerized accounting tools make it extremely easy to retrieve information on spending without maintaining hundreds of separate accounts to do it. Think about

---

13 Usually one refers to only five major balance sheet categories. I have added "reserves" as a sixth, and my preference is to treat it as a type of liability account. A good case can be made for treating it as an equity account instead, and I have no argument with those who wish to do so. In truth, some reserve accounts should probably be treated as liabilities because they consist of gifts given with a specific purpose in mind, which the congregation is bound to honor. Other reserves, such as building repair funds, are frequently created by the board from extra cash at year end. What the board has done in such a case can be undone; these are, truthfully, equity accounts. Some reserve accounts will have both special gifts and general revenues, and are a hybrid between equity and liability. I find it easiest for others to grasp quickly if they are all shown as a form of liability to some stated purpose.

the board meetings and committee meetings you have attended. Think about your chart of accounts. How much of that detail is being used? The IRS has a claim on certain types of information. Other than that, the rest is by your own design.

So, what is my design? The area of greatest flexibility, and requiring the most thought, is "expenses". If I were to start from scratch describing how the church spends its resources I would consider my most fundamental need first: expressing focus for the spending energies of the church. Fortunately this approach also has some relevance organizationally; usually the most useful way to organize people is also around the driving energies being expressed. There can be a duality between the "pure" programmatic expression of what we are about and the organizational manifestation. But, let's begin the thinking with a stronger focus on the programmatic description, rather than the organizational.

You will recall that we already identified the areas of energy when we discussed the process of raising funds. Remember too, while we need cleaning supplies for the kitchen we do not want to have the congregation focused on that need. Rather, we want attention paid to what it is that inspires us and gives meaning to our association several years into the future. These are the programmatic areas that make sense, to me at least.

lifelong spiritual exploration and growth

organizational health and leadership development

community presence and denominational support

membership support and pastoral care

To get the leadership and the congregation to agree on a vision in these areas, there will need to be in-depth planning and discussion about what they mean. This is the first purpose of the categories: stimulating thought and discussion about the purpose of being in community.

As that discussion begins to gel, various committees will see the direction in which they want to go. The budget grows out of such planning. Most committees will fit entirely and easily into one of these four categories. This is the second objective of my chart of accounts: to be supportive of committees and staff, to help them realize their importance to the whole.

The planning and envisioning categories arise from the rules of stewardship one adopts. Those above represent how I want to "see" my church, and how I want to encourage others to see it with me. (See Appendix 13 for an example of a chart of accounts.) I argue that they inspire and will raise more stewardship income than talking about the minister's housing allowance. In the last analysis, however, any account definitions are arbitrary. The only justification for them is that they will prove helpful in supporting my notion of stewardship, and that is clearly a judgment call.

Some will wonder, "What should we do with the minister's salary? It doesn't fit any category!" It's an excellent question with an ambiguous answer. A programmatic budget summarizes organizational "outputs" rather than "inputs." It is easiest to be definite about organizational inputs, such as salary, photocopying, postage, and telephone costs. It is difficult to categorize spending for outputs in a way that is entirely satisfying. How much of the choir costs are part of the worship program, and how much are they related to member involvement? There may be some arbitrary assignment of costs to more than a single account (like the minister's salary) Or, equally arbitrarily one can pull the minister and church secretary into a separate unallocated category: "General Operations."

As you review the chart of accounts, you will see that I have been arbitrary, but not capricious. While one must make a judgment about how to categorize the costs of the choir or of the family retreat, the judgment is not obtuse — whatever seems best to the leadership of the community is best. We are forgoing tidiness to come up with a financial picture of the community which, if vague on the edges, carries a deeper message.

Finally, as you review the specific Chart of Accounts offered in Appendix 13, you may notice that there are no committees listed, even though I have suggested the importance of supporting committees. Nomenclature that is descriptive of programs, rather than organizational entities, is preferable in my opinion because it reduces the tendency of groups to isolate themselves from the overall community. In small ways it is important to keep the notion alive that we are a single community, each part serving the whole.

Committees do have budgets and are responsible for administering them. They need to get routine budget reports showing how they are progressing through the year. Good software helps. Most committee functions are included within the chart of accounts, and can be coded to reproduce into a committee report.

Finally, it should be clear that the budget adopted by the board of trustees or the congregation may have a strong programmatic orientation. It might be more helpful to reformat that same budget for management purposes through the year. One might present a budget showing all the religious education costs, including salaries, as a single program area. Yet, in managing the budget it might be easier to have one category with all personnel costs: minister, RE Director, Music Director, teachers, community outreach workers, and so on. Reformatting the budget for administrative purposes is not a problem, as long as the leadership agrees.

RIGHT BRAIN ACCOUNTING

(with pictures!)

It is not necessary that you serve as Treasurer next year simply because you know a little accounting. If you are acquainted with the fundamental design of the accounting paradigm, however, you will have an easier time understanding the financial statements, will be able to comment intelligently on them at board meetings, and will follow the treasurer's train of thought. You will be better equipped as a congregational leader.

Why would anyone who professes an interest in the health of an organization want to remain unable to make an independent judgment about whether financing is in jeopardy? The accounting discipline developed over several centuries as part of the intellectual framework for the industrial revolution and the market economy. Indeed, the management and organization of large scale economic enterprise could not have happened without the development of accounting to organize economic data about organizations. Surely our church leadership, like other enterprise leaders through time, should grasp the fundamental concepts of the discipline.

In the next few pages, we are going to learn about the "Balance Sheet" (or Statement of Financial Position). The Balance Sheet is the foundation upon which further accounting is built. Then we will see how the "Income Statement" grows out of it. The Income Statement is a version of the budget report we usually get at board meetings.

These two financial statements provide the structure upon which we hang all accounting transactions. By gaining an understanding of the conceptual basis for these two reports, you will understand basic accounting. Then, in Appendix 14 you can walk through a few actual accounting transactions if you wish to see how the financial statements interact.

Let's start with the Balance Sheet, the foundation upon which accounting occurs. The Balance Sheet is a financial description of how your church looks at a particular point in time. (Professional accountants refer to it as the Statement of Financial Position, a more descriptive label.) It has three primary sections: Assets, Liabilities, and Accumulated Surplus.

BALANCE SHEET (Statement of Financial Position)	
Assets (color purple)	Liabilities (color red)
	Accumulated Surpluses (color blue)

Illustration 1

The assets are everything the church has such as money, investments, buildings, and equipment. The description of the church assets has no designation of purpose or obligation; they are just the things the church owns.

All the ownership characteristics of the assets are detailed on the other side of the Statement. Liabilities are existing claims against the Assets of the organization. Paying off all the Liabilities leaves the Accumulated Surplus. What we are referring to as "Surplus" would be called "net equity" in a business context. Some of the surplus resulted in prior year operations; some is from current year operations. Here is a Balance Sheet showing a little more detail in each of the main sections.

BALANCE SHEET (Statement of Financial Position)	

Assets
  cash
  checking account
  savings account
  investment account
  building
  land
	Liabilities
	  mortgage

	Accumulated Surpluses
	  prior years'
	  net of current year

Total, Assets xxx	Total, Liabilities & Accum. Surpl. xxx

Illustration 2

Graphically, you can see: Assets = Liabilities + Surplus

Or, more commonly: Assets - Liabilities = Surplus

The algebraic expression above *must always maintain its equality.* The "Balance Sheet" was named such historically because of this algebraic truth — the equation must always stay in balance. Every financial transaction, therefore, requires two entries. Sometimes there will be offsetting entries on each side of the equation; sometimes offsetting entries will both be made on one side of the equation. But, there must be two entries to keep the equality intact. Hence, the name "double entry bookkeeping". For example, one might move some cash from checking to savings – a plus and a minus to the asset side of the equation; or one might make a payment against the mortgage principal, reducing checking (an asset), and reducing the mortgage balance (a liability). Both these transactions involve two entries on the books, which keep the equation in balance. (Think about this before proceeding.)

Finally, there is one other important subdivision within the Accumulated Surplus section of the Balance Sheet. Some of the assets are for a designated purpose: either the donor or the board has specified an eventual use for the funds. They are "liabilities" in the minds of some, because of the restrictions placed on them. In truth however, these amounts are not legally owed to anyone other than the church. Thus, they are net assets "reserved" for some purpose. One could specify that the reserves from donors are liabilities and the reserves with only board or congregational designation are equity.

The trustees have an obligation to keep track of reserves to assure the purposes are met. They are "set aside" on the Balance Sheet rather than in a separate bank account. A common fear is that reserves might disappear if they are co-mingled with the other assets. However, the reserves are still available as long as there is sufficient liquidity to cover them, and positive fund balance.

Thus, a more complete Balance Sheet looks like this:

BALANCE SHEET	
(Statement of Financial Position)	
Assets	Liabilities
cash	mortgage
checking account	Reserves
savings account	organ fund
investment account	sabbatical savings
building	building repair fund
land	Accumulated Surpluses
	prior
	current
Total, Assets xxx	Total, Liab, Reserves, Surpl. xxx

Illustration 3

Conceptually you have seen what a Balance Sheet looks like. Now let's look at it in the more familiar format which you hope is attached to the Board agenda before you go to the meeting.

BALANCE SHEET	
(Statement of Financial Position)	
Assets	
Total, Assets	xxxx
Liabilities	
Reserves	
Surpluses	
total, Liabilities, Reserves, & Surpluses	xxxx

Illustration 4

As we noticed earlier, the Accumulated Surplus has two components. The amount designated as the "prior surplus" represents the unencumbered financial assets of the church community acquired from the beginning of time through the beginning of the current fiscal year. The "current surplus" is a one number summary of what has happened this year; it is the net result of all the money coming in and all the expenses this year. In fact, it is the same as the bottom line on our budget report. In the more formal language I used earlier, it is the net result showing on the Income Statement. In other words, we can add a second page behind the Balance Sheet — a "budget report" which expands that "current surplus" number to show the detail which is buried within it.

INCOME STATEMENT	
Revenues	
Expenses	
Net Surplus	net

Illustration 5

Notice how the "net" from the current year budget report fits into the balance sheet.

BALANCE SHEET	
Assets	
Total, Assets	xxxx
Liabilities; Reserves & Surpluses	
total, Liabilities	
total, Reserves,	
total, Accumulated Surpluses	
prior years's	
current year	net
Total Liabilities, Reserves and Surpluses	xxxx

In summary, we now know that the "balance sheet" or Statement of Financial Position is the basic starting place for understanding the financial affairs of an organization. It tells us at any moment in time just what the organization has in the way of debt, money in the bank, buildings, and money being held for some special purpose. The "net surpluses" are what could be left over if the organization closed down as of the date the statement is prepared. We know now that every financial transaction requires two entries on the "balance sheet". And, we know that if anything happens affecting the revenue and expenses this will be reflected on the income statement and carried over to the balance sheet too. For more understanding of how some accounting transactions work, see Appendix 14.

BORROWING TO BUILD

A capital campaign is different than a normal stewardship drive: the amount of money involved is larger by several times. It also is money that will be used on something that can be seen and touched. Thus, it is both more difficult and easier to finance capital needs. The main point is that it is different, so different that it needs different conceptual approaches, not simply more organization or more energy.

Let's approach this slowly: In order to build a building, we need cash. There are only two sources of cash for a church: loans or gifts.

Many congregational leaders have an aversion to loans. Usually the objection to borrowing is that interest costs are too high. Interest is a cost, but whether interest costs are too high depends on an assessment of the benefits of borrowing. Unfortunately, there is usually no weighing of benefits at all, so of course any costs are "too high".

There is sometimes also a fear that the congregation will borrow too much and get into trouble, perhaps even go into bankruptcy. Such a scenario does not happen often, but it does happen. And, when a church goes bankrupt or experiences extreme financial difficulty there is always debt present, by definition. Most churches that borrow, however, pay their debts. The more frequent problem is that after money is borrowed there is a continuing debt service that can crowd out the programmatic needs of the congregation. Sometimes there is a beautiful new building and no money left for what the congregation really needs.

The issue in such instances, then, is not borrowing *per se*, but ill-considered and excessive borrowing. Too huge a debt can cause a church to skimp on important program opportunities. Churches with debt also sometimes get into trouble for reasons quite apart from the indebtedness — such as a fissure within the community over the minister, or some other reason for commitments to evaporate. Even when debt is present, it is not always the culprit; sometimes it's a red herring. Let's clear a place in our minds to consider the possible benefits of church borrowing.

Three positive reasons to consider using loans

1) **It will be easier to pay for a new building as the congregation gets bigger.** Churches sometimes grow handsomely when a new building is built. A membership increase of 30% within three years is not uncommon, but neither is it guaranteed. It is difficult to accept this possibility when you're leading the congregation into the project. Other factors being equal, however, if you have a good demographic profile in your town, if you build extra capacity for newcomers, and if you build your church where it will be easily seen and found, the church will attract many visitors. If the congregation has vital and attractive programs, the visitors will become members. Where any one of these conditions is not present, long term membership growth is more problematic.

2) **More of the current members can participate in paying off the mortgage in a meaningful way.** Even for a congregation that believes it is stable and will not grow, there is something to be said for stretching the payments out over ten to fifteen years rather than three. If a building is to be completely paid for in three years, the congregation is necessarily leaning heavily on a few fortunate members who can afford to make sizable gifts from accumulated savings or very high incomes. In this scenario no one pays for the building after the three years are gone. By stretching out the payment schedule to a ten year period others are able to participate at a more moderate level out of current income rather than savings. They are more heavily involved in the project. Having a wider base of heavy participation is a worthy community goal.

3) **If a building mortgage is paid for over an extended time, new members get to participate in the costs too through their annual gifts.** Membership changes in a congregation over time even where there is little growth. Again, the widest possible spreading of support in paying for the building is the healthiest for the community. Extending the mortgage over several years ensures that all members who enjoy the use of the building also help finance it.

I noted above that there are two sources of cash — gifts and loans. In truth, there is only one source of cash. Ultimately any loans will also be paid off with gifts from members. Therefore the issue should be framed solely in terms of how those gifts are to be sought: quickly (primarily from wealthier congregants) or over a somewhat extended period (to include those who can only make gifts out of their income as they receive it).

A healthy congregation will assure that the widest array of members is involved in any capital campaign, and involved in a way that let's them know their participation mattered to the success of the project. Interest expense is not the cost to the congregation of borrowing money. Rather, it is the cost of obtaining that level of widespread participation in paying for new facilities. Such participation is healthy, making interest costs an important benefit, rather than an excessive cost.

There is still a legitimate need to determine how much debt a church can take on. It depends. There are many heuristic measures, each of which has some value, and some limitation. It is, in truth, a judgment which the leadership must make. It is a judgment based on determining 1) how much giving the congregation can do this year, 2) how much giving will unfold in the future if there are new members, and 3) how long the congregation will continue to give at the increased level. As I have tried to make clear earlier, I believe that Unitarian Universalists are capable of much higher giving levels than we generally expect.

Let's consider The Community Congregation again. This congregation has 218 committed pledging families or individuals and about 293 adult members. It is difficult to imagine a serious building project which would cost less than $1,000,000 for such a congregation. Suppose they can sell the current building and realize $500,000 in net cash. They are left with a need to seek gifts or financing for $500,000. Suppose further they decide to borrow the full amount, understanding that they will need to pay an interest rate of about 8%. The only remaining question is how long they will take to repay the loan.

If 5 years,	$125,000/year
If 10 years,	$75,000/year
If 15 years,	$60,000/year
If 20 years,	$50,000/year

The fundamental question the leadership faces is how much can be added to the current budget without endangering the ability of the congregation to still have the programs and services it wants. It is poor planning to build a religious education wing for example, then find that the church can no longer pay an RE Director.

But, as we see, such a situation is not entirely dependant on the amount of debt incurred. It is even more strongly a function of the expectations of the congregation in determining how long they must take to pay it off. Unless the congregation foresees its demise, there is much to be said for stretching out beyond ten years. The annual payments reduce substantially for each year of extension. Note that beyond twenty years, however, there is not much further reduction in the payment level.

Sources of capital funds

Those are the reasons for using borrowed money, best summarized as spreading participation in the financing to as many members as possible. Where do we get it? Banks will lend to churches, but (in my town) at higher rates than are applicable to second tier commercial loans. The denomination sometimes has money to loan at more attractive rates, but the amount available to any single church will usually not build much of a building. That means we must get a large portion from ourselves. Most of us have some savings in an IRA or in college accounts for the kids. This is not money available to give away; but it is available to loan for a few, or many, years.

There is a great deal of money in your own congregation! If you ask people to *give it to the church* you will never see it. If you ask people to *loan it and you agree to pay at least what the credit union is paying,* you can have all you want. Our congregations can come up with amazing amounts of cash by borrowing it from the members. A congregation I've been a member of raised $150,000 in loans in less than two weeks without much effort beyond an announcement in the newsletter and on Sunday morning. Other congregations have borrowed significantly more from members in a single weekend.

The Borrowing Campaign

Step 1: You will need help. **Call the District Office and get referred to someone who can do the technical legal work.** Borrowing money within the congregation requires very specialized legal work, usually including filing paperwork with the State under securities laws. Expect to pay for the attorney's efforts.

Step 2: Consider the various pools of cash you will be marketing to and structure the notes to be attractive to those needs. For example, retirees will want regular income and not much risk. This means some of the notes should be 4–5 years in duration, with an interest rate fixed for the entire period, and monthly or quarterly payments. For both college and IRA money, a series of notes maturing in 8, 10, or 12 years with a single payment at term is more attractive. These people may not want to be bothered with payments along the way. Interest can be adjusted annually (tied to something such as the ten-year Treasury bond rate), and compounded quarterly. There are diverse ways to set up your loan offerings. The point to consider is that there are a variety of needs of lenders. Structure terms appealing to the people who have the money.

Step 3: Do not go after loans and gifts at the same time! You will confuse your canvassers, and your members. They will get the message that after you have the money things will be like always. Someone will try to talk them into making the loan a gift. Do not fantasize about members "forgiving" the loans. When conducting a campaign to raise cash, make the effort entirely one of borrowing money — on terms that are attractive financially, seem secure to the lenders, and are straightforward in intention. (It is appropriate to invite members to forgive the loan in the event of their death. That is an option that can be offered with a simple initialing without endangering the perception of repayment under normal circumstances.)

In the quest for money to borrow, some will want to make an outright gift. That's what they want to do. It's always OK to take gifts, but a loan campaign must focus entirely on loans. After you have the loans set up there will be time to go after additional gifts later.

Step 4: Establish the appropriate financial controls to assure that the loans are dealt with responsibly every year in the budget. This means that each year an appropriate interest expense must be included in the budget as well as a set aside of a portion of the principal. Show a reserve account in the equity section on the Statement of Financial Position which is the "escrow" out of which note payments will be made as they are due. That's where all the interest expense and principal gets saved until it's needed.

Step 5: Organize a single canvass each year. It is important for the congregation to understand that the financial obligation of the mortgage is no different than the financial obligation of the minister's salary. Managing a separate canvass for each of these obligations makes no sense. It is clear that one well-done canvass is vastly superior to the draining sense that comes from running two or three major money raising events each year.

So, let's say we borrowed $500,000 in the fall. In the next regular annual canvass there is a major new item — debt repayment. It is not a negotiable item. It establishes the need for a higher commitment level from all the members, not just the ones who had savings to spare.

In every church budget I have reviewed, a standard of 5% in stewardship giving will provide enough to easily cover the operations of the congregation and to pay off capital notes. So, the annual canvass needs to focus on goals in the 3 – 7% range for all members.

There will be some in the congregation who want the loans "paid off as soon as possible". I believe this approach is wrong, in general, for the reasons outlined above (best summarized as spreading the cost to more people). And, if the terms of the notes are reasonably attractive, many of those who hold the notes will not want them paid off early either. After all, the members are getting an opportunity to increase their charitable contributions (to cover the larger debt costs) so that they can continue to receive attractive interest — often in their IRA accounts.

Carrying these notes has real benefits, if you can get the fiscal conservatives to turn around and consider them. Nevertheless, some will want to make gifts specifically directed to debt reduction. Here's my approach to such gifts: Note that the debt structure is pretty clearly spelled out in terms of due dates and interest rates. Every year anyone with a sharp pencil and a calculator can determine required escrow account reserves to meet the eventual payment obligations. If there is more than the required minimum in escrow, the church is ahead of schedule whether or not any cash payments are made.

Whenever a large debt reduction payment comes in, it should go directly into the escrow account. From that point on, the board should never let the escrow account fall behind on escrow overage.

For example, if a donation of $10,000 comes in to reduce the debt there is an opportunity to move the eventual debt payoff ahead by, say, six months. The promise I would extend to the donor would be that the payoff would not slip beyond that date again. This would guarantee that the church will be in a position to prepay all the obligations uniformly at a time earlier than promised. (No principal is paid at the time of the gift however; doing so would either violate the terms of the note for those who do not want prepayment, or violate the uniformity of treatment which should be extended to the note holders.) In the budget presentation there might be a footnote that clarifies this matter. For example: "The notes undertaken in financing the addition in 1995 are due December 1, 2010. Current escrow reserves are such that we will be able to pay these notes in full on June 1, 2009."

INTERNAL CONTROLS AND FINANCIAL OVERSIGHT

Aren't we all good people?

Over the past several years there have been numerous newsworthy events in which directors and managers of companies or not-for-profit organizations have been taken to task for failure to conduct the financial affairs of the organization soundly or responsibly. Some have gone into bankruptcy. This has given rise to serious revision of accounting rules and practices. Churches are not immune either to the new standards or to the expectation of increased scrutiny in the future.

What are some of these expectations?

First, every church should have financial policies and procedures, conflict of interest policies and "whistle blower" policies to which it adheres. The objective of such policies is to assure good operating practices while also preserving independent review of financial activity. A relatively new notion for churches to consider, "whistle blower protection" gives individuals a venue to voice a concern about something the treasurer, bookkeeper, minister or anyone else might be doing suspiciously and not face ostracism.

Every church, especially a larger one, should have a financial oversight function which is entirely separate from the finance committee. The job of the oversight committee is to periodically assure that expense transactions are authorized and recorded, that all income is accounted for, and that assets are safeguarded, including being insured as appropriate. A CPA is licensed to perform an audit or review. It is possible however for a financial oversight team to develop procedures to review such issues if a professional audit cannot be conducted every year. When a congregation is too small to have an independent oversight group a congregation's finance team can "trade" an annual review with a neighboring church. (It is not necessary that it be in the same denomination!) There is an example of oversight procedures in Appendix 17.

Finally, the finance committee needs to focus on internal controls. The term "internal controls" refers to the rules and processes we establish to ensure that the organization's money and property do not get lost, stolen, or misused. We do not install internal controls thinking at the outset that the people in our midst are embezzlers. We are a volunteer organization, however; and we have people who feel overworked and unappreciated, untrained, and who sometimes make errors. With any of us in such situations at 10:00 pm, dull faculties, anger, or other natural conditions of life can descend and lead us to wrong solutions to the problem at hand. Internal controls help to avoid the compounding of misunderstandings and errors. And sadly, it is also true that churches are among the prime targets of those who seek to embezzle precisely because church internal controls are notoriously lax.

Let's remind ourselves that any checks within a system will have flaws, will not catch everything. Unhappily, your church might hire a skilled bookkeeper whose primary intent is to fortify his or her income in an unauthorized way. A congregation will probably not do enough to detect this until after a large amount of money is gone. On the other hand, there are some fairly simple things that can be done to obtain 98% reliability against errors and misunderstandings, as well as making overt fraud much more difficult and early detection more likely.[14] As in all systems, the closer we get to perfection the greater is the cost of the effort involved.

The first rule is to not ask one person to do all the work. This seems pretty clear, yet is frequently ignored. I do not know whether UU congregations are typical in this regard, but there are not many in our midst who really enjoy keeping track of money and details. When we find someone with these tendencies, it is easy to load that individual with responsibility for the entire effort. "Burn out" is not the only reason to avoid this temptation.

So, two or three people take on some of the responsibility. Should they just "form a committee" and go do it? No! The second rule is to keep a clear delineation between financial tasks. Having two or three people sharing overlapping responsibilities throughout the financial system doesn't get us where we want to be. We'll look at specific ways to break down the financial management tasks below. Let's simply note the importance of reducing overlapping responsibilities. Even temporary "filling in" (during vacations, for example) by the same person who ordinarily is restricted from particular duties should be avoided if possible.

An example will make this clear. Many churches now use accounting software. All such reputable software has password protection built in. This means that the person who posts the payment transactions can be prevented from having

---

14 See in particular, Richard Vargo, Effective Church Accounting

the ability to make other entries to the books except from within the specific parameters of their function. [15]

If someone goes on vacation you would not then pass out their password to all the other users of the system, would you? Rather, you might see this opportunity to train a new backup person for that particular task during the vacation. The same principle applies whether or not you are using software. In this way you can preserve the separation of the functions, and also begin the process of recruiting and training replacement volunteers. Structure the problem as one of organizing the finance committee, which has three operating responsibilities.

1) **Taking in money and depositing it.** This can be a small group, at least two, who count and deposit money from stewardship receipts and the Sunday cash collections, collect rent, and establish value and issue receipts for donated items. These individuals can post income transactions to the books or complete and sign a weekly spreadsheet from which all such entries are recorded.

2) **Approving expenses and writing checks.**

    a. Every expense reimbursement must be approved by someone other than the check signer prior to the check being written. The finance committee must maintain a list of specific individuals who can authorize expenses (for example, staff members, ministers, committee chairs, and board members). Every expense needs to have a voucher which has both an approval signature and an indication of where it is to be charged in the budget.[16]

    b. There should be two or three authorized check signers; the check signers are *not* expense authorizers. With both an expense authorizer and a different check signer every expense is reviewed and approved by two people even though the check has only a single signature. The check signers are the individuals who can enter expense transactions on the books. For the sake of his or her reputation It is best if the minister is an authorizer, not a signer.

3) **Preparing and reconciling all reports and financial communications.** This important function must be carried out independently of the other

---

15 Use the password protection capability even though it may seem burdensome. This stuff is designed by people who have given more thought than you or I to creating systems with good internal controls of the sort we are discussing.

---

16 Sometimes a single voucher will authorize fixed payments for the year, such as rent or health insurance. In fact, many expenses are recurring and can be pre-approved for the year to reduce the burden of the process.

two. In smaller congregations it can be done by a single individual who is uninvolved in the other two activities, but it is easier to have more than one person.

a. An independent reconciliation of the monthly bank statements provides a check on the entry of both deposits and of expenses.

b. All stewardship reports to members should be prepared by other than those who record receipts; this provides a check on recording payments to appropriate individual records. This function might involve a small group who also do the in-person contact with members who fall behind.

c. Ideally the Treasurer should prepare reports of budget status to all committees, the board, and the congregation but is not directly involved in either recording receipts or expenses.

CASH MANAGEMENT

Every congregation has cash. Cash is whatever is available in the checking account to pay bills. There may be cash in other accounts too. "Cash" is anything that could be easily added to the checking account in less than a week. A CD at the bank can be broken, for example, and the funds added to the checking account. Stocks and bonds can be sold. These are not actions one might wish to take, but they can be accomplished easily and by doing so one can boost the checking account in a few days. In terms of "cash management" those are all forms of "cash".

Some congregations have a few people who worry there is not enough cash on hand; in other congregations many people worry there is not enough. In part this is a function of personality as much as it is of cash levels. We have different tolerance levels for the possibility of running short if "something happens".

The church Finance Committee needs to worry about cash sufficiency. There are two distinct ways to not have enough cash. First, a congregation may not have enough money on hand to meet its obligations, such as payroll, as they come due. This doesn't mean the church is bankrupt. Rather, it means that whatever the church has in the way of property or assets at that time is not liquid, not spendable, not Cash. The congregation might own the buildings and property outright, but not have any cash with which to pay bills.

The second way a congregation can be short on cash is more indirect and stealth-like. Suppose the congregation has reserve accounts totaling $100,000 but has Cash totaling $60,000. It is true that the congregation is not in the same situation as the prior example, yet most would agree that the cash situation is not healthy. For some reason the congregation has been borrowing, in effect, from the reserve accounts to meet current cash needs. There is nothing immoral and unhealthy in doing so, as long as the need is distinctly temporary, minor, and known. This example is probably neither. It is a situation that needs to be corrected, even though it does not present an emergency (as long as the reasons for holding reserves don't all manifest at the same time).

Let's discuss these situations as cases of the risk each presents. Consideration of risks is best done by isolating the causes. There three archetypes: the Working Capital Risk, the Contingency Risk, and the Nightmare Risk.

Working Capital Risk: The congregation has uneven cash flow. At some point(s) during the year more is going out than is coming in. A few months of that could happen even though the church is financially healthy in all other respects. There is simply a temporary negative cash flow, with more going out than coming in. It is anticipated, can be planned for, and controlled or eliminated.

Working Capital Risk is easiest to quantify. To do so, go through the financial reports for three (or more) years looking at every month in the period. Calculate the difference between the cash that came in each month and the cash that went out. Then, find the average change in cash level for the three Januarys, Februarys, etc.

Starting with the month your fiscal year starts add those averages together cumulatively in monthly order – July, July plus August, July plus August plus September, and so on for at least a twenty-four month period. (Start with zero.) You can graph these results if you wish for a visual understanding. This will tell you how far you might get in the hole with the cash flow as it usually presents itself in your church.

The biggest negative number you get to identifies your worst month for Working Capital Risk. Suppose it is -$5,000 in September. With that in mind, you know that you need to have about $5,000 in cash beyond the need to cover reserves as of the start of the fiscal year.

And, you can see that Working Capital Risk is normal. If you have had temporary cash problems of this sort they can be eliminated over a couple years by reducing spending to increase the checking account balance.

Contingency Risk: There are emergencies. Vandals bust a large picture window, for example. Termites are discovered to have eaten away a major section of the floor joists. The furnace stops working on Thanksgiving weekend. Risks of this sort face us all – the unexpected and sudden need to pay for something that represents a relatively large drain on our resources. Such events are likely to manifest, but we do not know when. Odds are good a church will experience Contingency Risk at least once in a five year period; such events are a virtual certainty in a ten year period.

Some churches have a Contingency or Emergency Fund for such occasions. Whatever the name, this is the risk being covered. And, it is a good idea to isolate the money saved for such emergencies in a separate reserve account. The congregation should be able to see it on the balance sheet.

How much should a congregation keep on hand in the Contingency Fund? There is not as clear a way to quantify this risk – and judgment rules. My own risk tolerance tells me 5% of the annual operating budget is sufficient. I would not go to the mat if some of the Board members felt 10% was more realistic.

(I might argue with them about the meaning of "realistic" when discussing risk; but, I would leave it at that.)

If one of the Board members argued, however, that an amount more than 25% of the annual budget, or "as much as we can possibly save" should be parked in a Contingency Fund I would curse and holler. My sense of congregational purpose tells me people do not give money to their church to protect against remote risks. Churches are called to do more important things in the world than sit on a big bank account.

If a congregation has a sufficiently large Contingency/Emergency Reserve and if all the reserve accounts are covered by available Cash, there is very little need to save any surpluses generated each year as budget savings. Such funds should be used to carry out the ministry.

Nightmare Risk: A financial nightmare may occur. I do not mean the difficulty we face every year in putting a responsible budget together. I mean instead an unforeseen shortage that will continue for several months, or several years. Suppose, for example, there is a congregational fissure and one-quarter of the members leave to form another congregation. Or, a windstorm causes major damage to your building. Or, global warming causes the oceans to rise 20 feet worldwide. Or, the water supply in ten major U.S. cities is ruined in terrorist attacks and millions die.

Many, many things could happen to cause financial nightmare for your congregation. Even if taken together they have a low probability of occurring, perhaps one or two in our lifetime. If such an event takes place it is disastrous at the time. But, the risk is not quantifiable. Further, it requires congregational response on many levels; financial difficulties, as great as they might be, are only part of the problem.

In short, with nightmare scenarios the possibilities are endless; the probabilities are remote; the problems will not be solved with a larger bank account. There are some who believe in their bones that churches should always budget to have a little left over, and should always add the surplus to savings. "You never know." Frequently our older members who grew up in depression era homes feel this way, and the feelings are understandable. But, rather than submit to an unbounded fear-based worldview, use your available resources to create sufficient working capital and a solid contingency fund. Then, create a vibrant congregation and a just world in this lifetime rather than a healthy bank account. Your congregation will be better for it.

REPORTING

Can we keep their eyes from glazing over?

The reason for preparing financial reports is to communicate with people. This suggests that the person preparing a report has something to say, or has responsibility for communicating something. Let's think about what it is the recipients want to know, and what we want them to know, and find the clearest way to say it. Particularly with numerical reports, there is no escaping the notion that as soon as we begin to summarize data we are taking on the responsibility for making useful interpretations of it.

Financial Reports

It is surprising how often church financial statements are visually cluttered, unclear, or incomplete. This frequent result happens in spite the well-intentioned treasurer naively offering every number anyone might ever want to see. Such "thorough" reports are prepared in an apparent belief that accuracy in detail is more important in financial statements than clarity of message. As a result board members sit around a table month after month looking at four or five pages of numbers, listening while the treasurer explains them, and still complain privately that they do not really understand what is happening. Treasurers are quantitative souls whose world is understood by the numbers. The others are usually not.

Good reporting makes financial people useful; interpretation and generalization of financial material is helpful. Overly detailed or disorganized reporting is dreadful and creates the sense that the organization is not well managed. Everyone loses confidence in an organization whose financial reporting seems in disarray. No one will offer wholehearted financial support in this environment. Even board members will commit less if the financial management is foggy. We need to find ways to make the numbers speak loudly and clearly.

Let's begin by describing the format of a well prepared financial report. A complete report from the treasurer contains three financial statements, each summarized on a single, separate page. We learned a little about the first two statements in Right Brain Accounting.

The Statement of Financial Position (balance sheet) will show where we stand right now. It will show how much is in the checking and savings accounts, the value of church property, how much is currently due on the mortgage, all the reserves which have been set aside, and the accumulated surplus or fund balance. It is a snapshot of the financial health of an organization at a single point in time.

The Statement of Current Activities (income statement or budget report) will show everything that has transpired thus far in the current fiscal year, usually juxtaposed with the budget to get a sense of whether the church is on target with its financial expectations. It is a longitudinal statement about the current year.

Finally, the Statement of Cash Flows contains information from each of the other statements. It will show the cash balance at the beginning of the year and all changes to get to the current cash position. "Cash" in this report usually includes items such as petty cash and savings certificates. (Whatever one decides to include or not include as "cash" must be the same for the beginning and end of the reported period, of course.) At the bottom of the cash flow statement I also include a calculation of the amount of "working capital" in the accounts, the amount beyond requirements to meet current liabilities and fulfill the requirements of the dedicated reserves. Here are some guidelines for preparing helpful financial reports. (See examples in Appendix 19.)

1) **Never prepare reports to the penny.** Never. Because humans do not absorb strings of digits well, we need to lop off the least meaningful of them. No one is interested in that level of accuracy, not even the members of the finance committee. (Offering reports at that level of accuracy trumpets amateurism on the part of the preparer.) The accounts must be kept to the penny, and computers do that fantastically well. But all reports get rounded to the dollar, at least.

2) **Some accounts get consolidated.** For example, you may be keeping track separately of a phone line dedicated to fax and computer, a monthly charge for internet access, an account for local telephone charges, and a separate account for a cell phone. When you report them, they can be summarized to "telephone and internet." Another useful area for consolidation is personnel expenses – benefits, employment related taxes, and so on. Where there are several paid staff members, there is no need to report to the board on the amount of salary, taxes, or benefits by individual employee. They need to be isolated in the bookkeeper's accounts, but in financial reports they can be summarized.

3) **Reports for different purposes have different numbers.** The budget prepared as part of the stewardship drive needs to be compatible with financial reports later in the year. They need not be identical because they are for different purposes. You will notice in Appendix 4, for example, that the vision budget for TCC lumps together interest expense, principal repayment, and other costs into the item "building and maintenance." Of course, principal repayments are not an expense and are handled differently in financial reports during the year. (See an explanation of this in Appendix 14.) None of us wants to stand before the congregation and explain how we need to pay down the mortgage principal, but it's not really an expense. It is easier to present the numbers in a format more easily digested.

Alternatively, some have argued that the stewardship drive budget might be better presented in the programmatic format I have suggested here. But, they argue, when it comes to expense control and authority during the year it is better to reformat to the traditional line items. If such control seems an important issue for you or your leadership through the year, I have no argument. The traditional line item budget is a singularly unimpressive, boring and nearly useless tool with which to engage the congregation however. One should design the format for the purpose at hand.

4) **Reports for different audiences are different.** When the finance committee, the board, and even the congregation all look at the same level of financial detail, one is drawn to the question, "why"? What issues are they each expected to deal with, and might that be more clearly understood with a somewhat different level of focus? If your church is large enough to have a finance committee in addition to the board for example, there should be an understanding between them regarding their different responsibilities, and the financial information they receive. The reason the board creates a finance committee is probably because they want closer scrutiny than the board provides. Thus, the board is asking for less detail, or less frequent reports, or both. If the board does not understand that as its request to the committee, then perhaps the board really wants a committee just to run the annual stewardship drive, in which case re-naming the committee might be in order.

5) **It can be helpful to vary the report information over the course of the year.** It might be that the financial report at the first few board meetings of the year would be oral only. There might be a written report to the board only quarterly for the first half of the year. Then the reports might be monthly for

the second half. Or particular items might be treated differently throughout the year. Stewardship income, for example, might be consolidated during the first six months; then it would be broken down between commitments made during the annual stewardship drive and those received from new members through the latter months of the year.

6) **Each financial statement needs to be confined to a single page.** This is an extreme statement to some, and reminiscent of a directive to the White House staff during the Reagan Presidency to never present an issue on more than a single page. But, consider the alternative. If the monthly "budget" report to the board is four pages of numbers, legal sized yet, it is worse than useless. It is dangerous because it creates the sense that the board knows what's happening. It is more helpful to reach toward the one page objective than to ignore it. The sample statements in Appendix 19 are only one page each. It is possible to provide useful reports in that format.

7) **Reports need lots of white space on the page.** If reports have more than four columns of numbers, the audience will be lost. The following four columns on the Statement of Current Activity describe everything the board might routinely want to know: 1) annual budget, 2) budget to date, 3) actual to date, and 4) variance to date.

8) **The numbers always need to be thoughtful and relevant.** Focus for a moment on the "budget to date" column mentioned above. Many reports which offer such a column heading use a straight line calculation, or a percentage of the year passed to calculate every number in the column. The assumption behind the calculation is that every income or expense item is evenly distributed through time, or that we wish it were. Do not fight reality on this point; many income and expense items are not evenly distributed through the year. Your report, to be most useful, must reflect reality.

Stewardship income, for example, is usually one of the more difficult items on the monthly report in which to have confidence. The community has fought hard to have a successful stewardship drive. Our experience tells us the income does not arrive in equal monthly increments however. Since stewardship income is usually the largest single source of support, we can be left wondering all year whether we will end up "on budget". Let's give particualr attention to this number.

There are patterns of giving which repeat year after year. The gifts the church receives are affected by tax season, summer, and so on. It is helpful to study the actual patterns occurring in your congregation; it will give you a stronger sense whether stewardship commitments are on target or not as the year progresses.

It may be that your chart of accounts and historical adherence to it make it very easy to determine the rate at which total stewardship receipts have been paid historically. I try to keep stewardship income in three separate categories for accounting purposes: 1) payment against commitments made during the stewardship campaign; 2) payments on stewardship commitments made later, either by new members mid-year or by others who didn't get around to pledging during the canvass drive; and 3) payments made late by either group, after the end of the fiscal year for which intended.

If you have those categories, great! The first question to address: How much of the amount that is pledged during the canvass can we realistically expect to receive during the following fiscal year? Pull out the payment histories on 20% of the pledging families or individuals each year for three or four years – a different selection each year, but all from those who made a commitment during the stewardship campaign. Find a way to do this randomly. You do not want to choose only people you know, or like (or don't like!). You simply want to find the total pledged by a representative group and how much of their commitment was actually paid eventually.[17] Break out the percentage paid in twelve months, and the increment paid late.

After doing this you can make a confident guess as you take the stewardship campaign total to the budget meeting. You can offer two pretty good numbers – the amount of the stewardship pledge total you can count on this year, and the amount of late pledge payments you can expect both this year and next. In my congregation we count on getting about 92% of the canvass commitments during the year and an additional 3% during the first three months of the following year.

Once you have determined how much stewardship income you are likely to receive in total you will still want to know what to expect as a likely rate

---

17 I have left out those who committed less than $200/year when I did this in my congregation – on the supposition that "information" provided by that group would have negligable impact on the results. I also note that I did not worry excessively about having overlap among the different groups – I weeded out a few heavy repeaters however.

of monthly receipts. It is best, I think, to use gross averages for this rather than averaging together the behaviors of particular individuals. So, it is a less complex problem:

a. Get copies of all the monthly financial reports for the past three years. Copy the cumulative receipts by month for all those years onto a spreadsheet. If you have reports showing only the gifts from the canvass commitments, use those; otherwise use what you have.
b. Add together all the receipts through July, through August, through September, and so on. This eliminates distortions caused by occasional five week months.
c. Calculate the percentage of the total for each month. You will end up with a series of numbers like 12% 17%, 24% 30%, ...etc
d. Apply those percentages to the total income you expect to receive actually, not to the total commitments.

Make a similarly thoughtful calculation with other expense categories too if you wish. Some staff, for example, may be paid year around; others may be paid on a ten month basis. Many RE expenses occur in the same months every year because that's when the DRE orders most supplies. It makes no sense to compare actual spending in such instances to an irrelevant number which distributes the budget evenly throughout the year.

Stewardship Reports

Rarely is the "report on the stewardship drive" more than the repeating of a single number to the Trustees and to the congregation: How much is the gifts commitment this year? The answer to that one question is held up as either indicative of success, or failure. What congregants decide to contribute to their congregation is a terrific indicator, however, of a congregation's gestalt and ministerial health. Surely we might learn something more if, after the stewardship drive is over, we look at the results a little more closely.

There are two ways to study data after the stewardship drive – one can compare a given congregation with others that seem pretty similar, or one can compare a congregation's results with what has happened with that same congregation in years past. Both kinds of analysis can yield useful information in theory. My own preference however is to spend more time and energy thinking about what happened in our congregation this year vs. what has been happening in prior years. There are two reasons to be a little wary of comparisons across different congregations. First, while two congregations may seem similar, they are never so. One can make crude comparisons regarding the number of members, or staff, or whether they are in the same community, but factors not as easily comparable are most important in determining member support. So, while one can say the average commitment here is such and such amount, as compared with this other church, after making the comparison one does not know, nor can one easily determine, why. Thus, one is left with numeric comparisons without insight – which have questionable value.

Second, when one is looking at a single congregation over a number of years, one has more control over the collection and manipulation of the data. For example, does the "average commitment" amount include the zero commitments? Does it include only those commitments received during the annual stewardship drive? Is it computed as a per member number or a per family number? The difficulties of maintaining consistency over the years within a single congregation are considerable; they are more onerous when comparing different churches.

Having said this, there is still some value in congregational comparisons. If, for example, your church has a "similar" sister church in the next town and you learn that the average commitment is double what yours is, or even 50% higher, that's enough of a discrepancy that it might be useful to explore it further. This does not mean simply accepting the unfavorable comparison and exhorting your own members to "do like they do" in the next annual drive. Rather, the leadership of the two congregations might pursue the apparent difference through discussion.

When thinking about what kind of year to year changes might be important to the leadership of a congregation, I suggest the following data at a minimum: How many new committing families or individuals are there? How many have disappeared, or stopped? How many have decreased giving by more than $25/month? How many have increased giving by more than $25/month? What is the median percentage change in stewardship commitments (note: not the median dollar change)? How are these changes in commitment distributed among the large, medium, and small givers?

I have included a sample stewardship history report in Appendix 21. The annual budget drive team needs to prepare such a report to be shared with the leadership every year. After collecting such data for three years or more, you will be able to detect trends or expectations. It becomes clear in reviewing the report what kind of follow-up might be called for, where the weaknesses and strengths of giving are in your congregation.

You will notice in my sample report (Appendix 21) I have segmented families and individuals into giving groups by dollar amount. While you might prefer to conduct a stewardship drive with recognition levels using percentages, when analyzing stewardship giving (which has a very limited audience) use hard dollar information for increased accuracy. I divide stewardship giving families into quartile groups. That is, I arrange all the families or individuals from largest commitment to smallest. Then, I add the gifts from the top and work down until I get to about 25% of the total. That's the first quartile. I continue down until I find the group giving the next 25% of the total, and so on. The reason for this more detailed level of understanding is to set aside the "noise" introduced by the lowest level givers. As a group you will find that their stewardship has a life of its own, and they are not subject to the trends of higher level givers. Your discernment regarding the primary supporters will be more informed if you break away from overall averages.

FINAL THOUGHTS

We began this conversation considering church financial management as part of the context within which our spiritual communities grow. We have thought about *stewardship* in our religious communities as more than learning about how to keep track of financial transactions; it is also about supporting Right Relationship.

As a steward in my church and in the denomination, I am partly responsible for our future. So are you. As you have reflected on stewardship and thought about the way your church manages its financial affairs, you may have discovered something you'd like to do better. My hope is that each reader will become an actor — that you will take a minor part and bring quality to your scene. We'll each do it again, and again, and again. From a series of well-crafted scenes, we'll fashion a great play.

Each of us can embrace the job we take on: improve upon the way it was done in the past, understand it as more rather than less important to the community, become stewards rather than custodians. We'll make some small changes this year and improve more next year.

The good news is that our efforts are noticed. Others see that we care about the way they understand the budget and that we are a little less desperate when revenue slips (as it does) in August. In addition to talking about the carpet that has not been cleaned in the past five years, some of the congregants are talking about a search process for a new campus ministry start-up in about two years. The low grade infection, the funk, that has hung on begins to dissipate; the lethargy begins to lift; the spirit is renewed.

Appendix 1
Financial Policies

THE COMMUNITY CONGREGATION
FINANCIAL POLICIES

2010:   This policy governs the financial operations of TCC, all its committees, and all affiliate organizations which use the financial accounts and record keeping services of the congregation.

2011:   The fiscal year of TCC is July 1 through June 30.

2100:   Assets

2110:   There should be free cash surpluses (working capital) at the beginning of each fiscal year equal to 5% of the budgeted spending level, providing protection from the effects of uneven cash flow as well as cushioning for possible budget shortfalls. Excess working capital beyond 5% may be transferred to other reserve accounts as directed by the Board. When cash surpluses are not sufficient, it shall not be necessary to recover the entire shortage in a single year, but progress toward that objective will be included in the proposed budget. That is, the proposed budget will project a surplus whenever working capital is lower than the policy standard.

2200:   Liabilities

2210:   Loans of less than $5,000 may be taken on behalf of the congregation by the Board for periods intended to be less than 90 days. Any loan in excess of this amount or for an extended period must be approved at a congregational meeting.

2220:   All outstanding loans shall be included in the proposed budget with a reasonable interest rate and amortization of principal.

2300:   Revenue

2310:   An objective of the Board over time is to identify the core programs and operations of TCC, and to finance them with generalized sources of income, primarily stewardship gifts. The premise of the annual stewardship drive is that

Members will participate generously. Thus, any particular program which is understood to be part of the core operation of the congregation shall have a diminishing reliance on special, dedicated funding

2315:   All fundraising other than the stewardship drive will be presented as an additional opportunity to participate in a worthwhile activity or worthy cause. While these special designated supportive funding sources are not in the core operating budget, they are reported in the financial statements during the year so that the congregation and its leadership can see the full financial impact of TCC operations.

2320: Only with rare exception will there be a special appeal for a budget shortfall or for emergency purposes.

2370:   Stewardship contributions must be in cash or negotiable securities unless specifically exempted by the Board of Trustees. A stewardship commitment may not be discharged by performing volunteer work for the Fellowship or by donating goods of services.

2400:   Expenses

2500:   Reserves and Accumulated Savings

2510:   Reserve accounts are established to hold special designated gifts and amounts set aside for a specific future use. Reserve balances may build up over several years. The spending of reserves is not governed by the annual budget but rather by the convenience or timing of the particular purpose.

2511: Reserve accounts are established only by the Board, only for a designated purpose, and only with specific assignment of responsibility for authorizing expenditures. When establishing reserve accounts for designated gifts the Board will remain cognizant of the wishes of the donor(s). However, the Board has prime authority over all reserves and may change the character of reserves as its judgment dictates.

2512: If there are sub-accounts maintained within a particular reserve category at the request of the responsible committee or individual, their judgment in transferring funds between the sub-accounts is authorized.

2513: Designated Reserve Accounts:

a) **Worship Aesthetics Fund:** For the purchase of permanent aesthetic enhancements for our worship services such as table coverings, chalice, and podium panel. Funds are not to be used for temporary or seasonal purposes such as flowers. Use of this money will be directed by the Worship Committee.

b) **Pre-paid Stewardship commitments:** This is a temporary reserve for holding payments made prior to the beginning of the fiscal year. It is for the exclusive use of the bookkeeper. Most years the fund will have a zero balance within 30 days of the start of the fiscal year, until the next annual budget drive.

c) **CapitalRepair and Replacement:** For non-standard major maintenance, repair, and upgrading of the buildings and the systems within the buildings. Used for items not normally anticipated as ongoing annual expense. Typical uses are roof repair, electrical wiring replacement, heating system repair, audio system improvements, remodeling, and building leakage repair. Typical of annual expenses not eligible for reserve use are interior painting, bug extermination (but not repair), carpet cleaning, shelving, and so on. These funds may be used as necessary by the Buildings and Grounds Committee, except that projects larger than $2,000 must have Board concurrence.

The Finance Committee and the Board intend to present a proposed budget to the congregation each year which includes at least 2% of the balance sheet value of the church buildings transferred to Repair & Replacement Reserves.

d) **Make the World a Better Place:** For gifts to organizations which enhance TCC values in the community or in the world, supporting environmental improvement, social justice, or social action. It is funded by designated worship offerings as well as special fundraising projects. Use of funds will be directed by the Social Action Committee.

e) **Emergency/Contingency Financing:** For major unanticipated events such as an unexpected shortfall in stewardship income. This Fund shall not be included in the proposed budget as a balancing item however. Contingency expenses are authorized only by the Board except that the Administrative

Vice President may approve emergency expenses and notify the Board subsequently

f) **Future Search**: Funds collected to defray the eventual costs associated with ministerial and professional staff search. Funds are spent only with Board approval.

g) **Landscaping:** This reserve account includes funds for enhancements to the grounds surrounding the buildings. They can be used for any outdoor purpose. The funds are used as needed by the Grounds Committee. Any project in excess of $2,000 however requires the concurrence of the Board.

h) **Late Expenses:** This is a temporary reserve account for the exclusive use of the Bookkeeper. If there are known outstanding expenses at year end they may be expensed into this account until valid documentation is presented for payment. All such expenses are to be paid out before October 1, or the balance credited back to the then current budget creating a zero reserve balance between October 1 and the following June 15.

i) **Leadership Development Fund:** To support members of the congregation or regular hourly staff in attending denominational gatherings, leadership training, or skill development courses within the normal operation of the church community (for example: renaissance module training for Religious Education teachers, leadership school, software training and so on). As a result of the use of these funds there must be a direct impact on congregational operations. Proposed expenses will be approved by the Board with advice from the Minister.

j) **Minister's Sabbatical:** Savings set aside to defray extra costs incurred during periods when the minister is on sabbatical. Funds are expended by the Worship Committee.

k) **Music Fund:** Gifts to the Music Fund may support the repair or tuning of the piano or chimes, the purchase of music, or any other item supportive of the music program at TCC. The Music Committee may use the funds as appropriate. Any Music Fund expense in excess of $2,000 must be reviewed and approved by the Board.

l) **REPlayground Equipment:** These funds are for the enhancement or repair of the playground. Use is determined jointly by the RE Committee and the Landscaping Committee.

m) **REPrograms and Training**: This fund includes income from annual wreath sales as well as gifts. It is used to enhance RE curriculum activities and programmatic needs as well as teacher training or appreciation gifts up to $25 in value. Its use is directed by the Director of Religious Education with advice from the RE Committee.

n) **RE Social Action:** This fund is for gifts raised by the children through Sunday offerings, Guest at Your Table, UNICEF Trick or Treat, and similar opportunities for developing generous supportive values and attitudes. The funds are used to support UNICEF, UUSC, and other organizations as determined by the children and the DRE.

o) **YRUU:** This fund is for gifts as well as funds secured by the youth in their fund-raising activities. The funds are used to defray costs of high school group youth attending events such as regional or District youth gatherings, General Assembly, ConCon, and so on. The funds may be spent by agreement among the three designated officers of the youth group and the Youth Advisor(s), with no more than one of those persons disagreeing with the proposal.

2600: Budget Development Process

2601:   The development of an annual congregational budget each year can be a catalyst for bringing focus on longer term priorities and interests, in addition to the necessity of incremental allocation of next year's resources. To that end, it is the expectation of the Board that the Administrative Vice President will use a process that includes discussion and planning input from a broad range of MSUUF leadership and staff.

2610: Budget Calendar

2611:   **October** – The Program Council and the Board hold a joint meeting to consider the Developmental Plan. In each major program area the participants should discuss how the congregation's mission is being served, the general objectives for each major program, and specific activities that would enhance our ability to attain those objectives. The discussion should assume a congregational growth rate of about 5% and a stewardship commitment growth rate of 10% to create a context for expansive thinking.

2612: **November/December** – Committees spend time discussing future programs and opportunities at their own meetings to bring forth specific ideas for the following two or three years. Relevant staff should be included in committee deliberations.

2613: **January:** The Program Council meeting is devoted to discussion of specific plans and ideas to move the congregation ahead during the next two to three years. This is an open-ended discussion during which committee chairs and staff can share ideas, looking for overlap and interaction among programs and projects. All staff members are strongly encouraged to attend and participate in this discussion. The meeting should not be distracted by any of the usual Program Council month to month issues. Generally, this is not a meeting that Board members should attend.

2614: **Late January** – The Administrative Vice President will deliver data on the current budget broken into program, committee, or staff responsibility areas. Every program area has a committee or staff person assigned lead responsibility for articulating needs and desires.

2615: The following items must be included in committee or staff submissions for budget development consideration.

a. Title and/or brief descriptive reference for proposal.
b. Dollars requested for next year with line item breakdown.
c. Explanation of how the proposal moves MSUUF toward accomplishing specific program objectives or mission/vision goals.
d. Description of increased spending that would be required or desired to further enhance the program objective over the next three to five years.
e. A description of how the cost estimates were arrived at. If the estimates are a "guess" include an indication of what factors inform the guess.

2616: **Mid- to Late February:** Budget requests and needs statements from staff and committees come to the Administrative Vice President. She/He assembles three sets of material to be distributed at the March Board meeting.

a. A reasonable projection of membership, pledge unit, and average monthly pledge growth levels anticipated four years into the future.

b. A base expenditure budget which projects the cost of current program requirements four years into the future at a general level of estimating. Using the income projections, a crude notion of excess or shortage in available resources, is derived.

c. Specific proposed program increases for the next budget year with costs also projected into future years. These are all items about which a "yes or no" decision will be made eventually. Nothing that has been requested by staff or committees should be hidden from Board consideration; each item proposed by staff and committees is either in the base budget or on the list of desired additions.

2617: **Mid-March** – The Board holds a special **Budget Priority Meeting**. The primary task at this meeting is for the Board to clarify priorities regarding new initiatives and to rank the additive items into priority groupings of roughly similar cost magnitude. Staff and committee chairs should be encouraged to attend.

a. *High Priority*: Recognition of prior commitments or additions which if not made will severely cripple existing programs.

b. *Medium Priority:* Items that are clear enhancements to our mission and/or are cost effective.

c. *Low Priority:* Items which would tend to enhance our mission, but can be deferred without jeopardy to it.

d. *Other Funding:* Items for which it is reasonable to expect financing can be obtained outside the normal operating budget.

No final decisions are made at this time. However, given the tentative priority rankings the Trustees will choose some of the items for inclusion in the following year Vision Budget. This generalized list and the associated cost parameters will be delivered to the Stewardship Drive Leadership Team.

2618: **Mid- to Late May** – The Administrative Vice President brings the Board an updated best guess regarding next year's income based upon the completed Stewardship Drive and the estimated end of year working capital level. The Board concurs or changes the income and growth estimates. The "bottom line" thus derived indicates how deep into the prioritized list from the March discussion will focus. Because the budget format is multi-year the Board can also gain perspective on budget issues that may occur subsequent to the first year.

2619: **June – Annual Congregational Meeting**: The budget year begins July 1. The congregation is required to consider the budget and this is interpreted by tradition to mean it will be voted on at the Annual Meeting in June.

Appendix 2
Employment Philosophy

The Community Congregation

STATEMENT OF EMPLOYMENT PHILOSOPHY

1. Our employment philosophy is grounded in the Principles and Purposes of the Unitarian Universalist Association.

2. We are respectful of the worth and dignity of all persons. People will be hired and employed by TCC on the basis of ability, experience, character, and attitude without regard to age, gender, affectional preference, race, national origin, creed, religious affiliation, or marital status. Nor will anyone be rejected for employment on the basis of physical disabilities, so long as they are able to perform the necessary functions of the position. The congregation may require familiarity with the culture and dynamics of UU congregations or the history of our religious movement for some positions.

3. It is the intent of TCC that staff will have a long term relationship with TCC, that their employment with us will offer personal satisfaction and growth, and that the relationship will be mutually rewarding.

4. Every salaried or regular hourly position will have a description of duties and expectations as well as an established compensation scale or range based upon the contribution of the position to the overall ministry of the congregation. Compensation will be determined on the basis of sound business practices and economics in the local community as well as attention to guidelines recommended by the UUA for similar positions in similar sized churches. Staff will be paid (beginning July 1, 2005 at the latest) within the established range. All jobs will be reviewed at least every three years to assure the responsibilities are clear and fit within the current employment and volunteer profile.

5. Anyone employed on a salary basis, or hourly more than 1,000 hours/year, will have the following benefits available for purchase: group dental, term life, and disability insurance. The cost of disability insurance will be shared 50/50 by the congregation; the others will be paid by the employee. The same employees will receive medical insurance with TCC participating at least 50/50 in the cost. The same group will receive wage based contributions to a retirement plan after 12 months employment in such a position. All staff working more than 500 hours/year will have holidays and vacations under an established schedule and paid by TCC pro-rata based upon time worked. All the benefits outlined in this section are not currently available but the

package indicated above will be fully implemented within three years of adoption of this Statement of Employment Philosophy.

6. We will provide an office and work environment which is orderly, safe, and comfortable. Every person employed by TCC will know who their supervisor is, or where to turn for coaching, support, resolution of grievances and other conditions of organizational employment. Harassment or intimidation will not be tolerated.

7. The Minister and the Board will give full, fair, and prompt consideration to any complaint that may arise in the employment environment. All staff persons are encouraged to suggest improvements in the way work is performed, and we expect them to be full partners in performance evaluations.

Appendix 3
Requesting Committee Plans

The Community Congregation
ADULT LEARNING AND OUTREACH MINISTRY
2009

Congregational Covenant Statement: To support members of the congregation in lifelong spiritual growth, to promote democratic processes and justice in all human relationships, to manifest the UU Principles and Practices in our lives and in our communities, and to encourage others to share in our liberal religious values.

Committee Mission: To assist adults in the church and in the larger community in developing their spiritual awareness, their self understanding, and their relationship capabilities.

Board Comments: The Board has adopted an expected growth rate for planning purposes. We currently have 218 pledge units and 293 members. Within three years we expect to have 250 pledge units and nearly 350 members. Part of that growth will result from the continuation and expansion of the fine work your committee has been doing with Lifespan Learning offerings.

How will your committee be affected by our growth?

What do you need to do to be successful in helping adults discover and develop their faith? What is the current profile of those engaged in courses: Singles? Young Adults? Long time members? What must we do to make our adult programs attractive and embracing to all?

Committee Response and Plans: (Most committees will feel better about communicating their plans if they are given an opportunity to describe them verbally. Do not make the mistake of thinking that because you want numbers, numbers are all you should ask for. Do not allow them to think that because you want numbers, numbers are all you need.)

Financing required for next year:

Financing required in three years:

Appendix 4
Vision Budget

THE COMMUNITY CONGREGATION
FINANCIAL PLAN & BUDGET
FISCAL YEAR 09/10
(dollars in thousands - draft 3/9/2009)

	08/09 estimated	budget 09/10	projected 10/11	projected 11/12	projected 12/13
Budget Drive Commitments	197	208	220	230	250
Average Monthly Commitment/Unit	84	90	110	125	145
Ave. % Stewardship Gift (reported/projected)	1.3%	1.5%	1.8%	2.1%	2.5%
REVENUE (total)	**245.1**	**326.6**	**337**	**400**	**500**
total stewardship & gifts	195.3	222.9	275	330	435
total sales, fees, and fundraising	19.7	42.7	25	25	15
endowment & misc. income	30.1	61.0	37	45	50
EXPENSES (total)	**235.4**	**322.5**	**345**	**409**	**480**
worship & faith development	*117.2*	*159.7*	*180*	*190*	*230*
worship and adult learning	88.3	118.2	125	130	135
ministry for children & youth	28.9	41.5	45	50	60
South County College, campus ministry	0.0	0.0	10	10	35
organizational devel. & operational support	*97.1*	*122.6*	*104.4*	*106.7*	*113.5*
board, training, travel	4.8	1.2	5	6	6
stewardship, finance and personnel ops.	2.6	0.8	3	3	3
office expense	7.8	6.8	8	8	8
office staff	47.1	55.0	39	39	42
utilities, building, maintenance	26.0	47.8	39	40	43
xfer to Leave Liability Reserves	0.8	1.0	1	1	2
xfer to Repair & Replacement Res.	6.0	8.0	8	8	8
xfer to Sabbatical Reserves	2.0	2.0	2	2	2
membership support	*5.6*	*15.2*	*19.2*	*25.2*	*30.2*
newsletter / advertising / web	*4.0*	*4.1*	*8*	*8*	*8*
membership services & hospitality	0.9	0.9	1	1	1
retreats & fun raisers	0.7	1.2	1	1	1
pastoral services	0.0	9.0	9	15	20
community presence & denom. mission	*15.5*	*25.0*	*41*	*87*	*106*
Living Oaks Retirement Cent./ hospice	0.0	0.0	2	35	48
individual assistance and org. support	1.5	1.0	9	12	16
UU Service Committee	0.0	0.0	4	7	7
Transylvania Sister Church	1.0	0.8	2	8	10
district & denominational support	13.0	23.2	24	25	25
NET TO WORKING CAPITAL	**9.7**	**4.1**	**-8**	**-9**	**20**

Appendix 5
Membership Standards Bylaw

MEMBERSHIP

We welcome everyone to worship with us and to benefit from our ministries without regard to faith journey, race, age, cultural background, sexual identity, or affectional preference.

I. A **Member Friend** of The Community Congregation must:
a) Attend worship at least four times during the prior year.
b) Sign the Membership Book in the presence of a Minister or Trustee. This is frequently accomplished as part of the final ceremony of the Meaning of Membership Course (MOM).
c) Engage with the church community in harmony with the Principles and Purposes of the Unitarian Universalist Association.

II. Only **Stewards** may serve as head of a ministry team or committee, teach in the religious education program, vote at congregational meetings, or hold elective office in the church. After 90 days as a Member Friend and by meeting these additional criteria the Board will confer the status of Steward:
a) Attain the 18th birthday.
b) Within the past three years complete the ten month Meaning of Membership course offered by the Membership Services Committee. Those under 21 may meet this requirement alternatively through recent regular participation in the Youth Group program.
c) Be present in the life of the congregation regularly based upon such considerations as attending Sunday worship, serving on a TCC committee, assisting in the religious education program or participating in one of the service ministries.
d) Meet one of the following conditions of financial support:
   1) Individuals or families attesting to the Senior Minister or Board President to an income of less than $10,000/year are not required to commit to ongoing financial support. An identifiable financial contribution of any amount is required during the six months prior to a congregational meeting however. Those under the age of 25 and financially dependant on their parents are not required to consider their parents' income.
   2) Individuals or families who do not attest to an income of less than $10,000/year must make a stewardship commitment to maintain at least Supporting Member status as established in the current Giving

Guide, and not be more than ten months in arrears at the time of a congregational meeting.

III. At least in January and July the Treasurer and the Membership Services Committee Chair shall jointly sign and deliver to the Board a list of Stewards, noting additions and deletions, and the Board will review and affirm the designations. The Board may waive any of the above criteria on an individual case basis in consultation with the Senior Minister in a closed meeting.

IV. Stewards must wear their nametags to membership meetings to vote.

Appendix 6
Budget Drive Calendar

The Community Congregation
ANNUAL BUDGET DRIVE
GENERAL PLAN

A. Multi-Year Calendar. There are different formats for the annual stewardship drive, each with different strengths. The TCC Board wishes to rotate through three types on a regular cycle in the following order:

Year 1 – Celebration Sunday or a similar Big Event with the entire congregation present in one body. We see an advantage in having our congregation celebrate our generous tendencies as a single group from time to time.

Years 2 through 4 – Personal Face-to-Face meetings with canvassers meeting members in their homes, over coffee for example. The advantage and objective of this format is engaging in personal conversations about the congregation's strengths and weaknesses and giving each person an opportunity to give voice to what is important for their own growth within our spiritual community.

Year 5 – Small Group Gatherings involving dinner meetings in member homes or similar venue with at least one recognized leader present at each gathering (e.g., the Minister, Director of Religious Education, a Trustee, or leader of the Stewardship Team). The objective in these years is to encourage members in talking among themselves about what they hope for in the future of the congregation, and to have such conversations inform leadership.

B. Annual Calendar. We request adherence to the year around calendar for planning purposes. Of course the dates will always be modified for the current year plan, but the following parameters should serve as guide.

Summer Board Meeting: Board receives a **Stewardship Drive Wrap-Up Report**. The **Board discusses the report** with the prior Leadership Team, including the designated Budget Drive Chair for the following year.

By September 1: Leadership Team selected for the next Budget Drive.

October: The Leadership Team (4 – 5 people) should **outline major tasks** and the time frame for completion of each. The tasks will vary depending on the format, but not in the timing.

November 1: Begin recruiting canvassers, dinner hosts, or other major task leaders. If canvassers are needed, plan on 25% of the current number of pledge units in the role of canvassers (including Leadership Team). This assumes you will have a list of prospects somewhat longer than simply current pledgers.

The following schedule is more specific to the Face to Face solicitation format. Other years will vary slightly.

First Week in January: Annual Budget Drive Chair, Treasurer and Membership Chair, **develop the firm list** of those who will be solicited during the drive.

January 15 – February 15: Gather information and print two cards for each pledge unit. Cards should contain the following information:

> Card 1: Name, Address, Phone
> Indication of membership status
> Names of children, whether in the religious education program
> Status of current stewardship commitment

> Card 2: Only the pre-printed name varies
> Information regarding the current canvass
> Space for making monthly commitment
> Indicate choice of payment schedule
> Signature line
> Area for notes

Note: This information is sensitive and the cards should be shared only between the Budget Drive Chair, Team Leader, and Canvasser.

March: Canvasser training should be scheduled on at least three alternate dates. Every canvasser, even if experienced, must attend a current year training session. At the training review the congregational vision, goals, and priorities in the next budget. Practice.

Last week in March: The Leadership Team hosts a **Kickoff Party/Gathering**. The Board, Leadership Team and the top ten givers attend. (Total group, including spouses will probably be 25.) Schedule Stewardship Commitment meetings for the entire group during the following week.

Second week in April: Stewardship Drive Kickoff is announced at the Sunday morning services. Tell the congregation where we are with the stewardship commitments from the advance group. Lunch after the second service is attended by the Leadership Team and all canvassers. At the lunch each canvasser receives the following:

> Canvassers Guidebook
> Stewardship Vision Budget
> List of questions and answers on pledging
> List of conversation starters
> Suggested Giving Chart
> 2 cards for each family or individual to be visited
> EFT authorization forms

April 15 – 30: General Stewardship Drive

April 20 (Thursday evening): Team Leaders **check-in** with canvassers by phone.

April 22 (Saturday morning): Mid-Point check-in at church. Coffee, donuts, and coaching will be provided by the Leadership Team. Completed cards returned.

April 27 (Thursday evening): Team Leaders **check-in** with canvassers by phone.

April 29 (Saturday Late Afternoon): Final Call. Return all Commitment Cards! Leadership Team members are all present to thank canvassers. Each Team Leader is responsible for making sure all cards will be returned. If a canvasser will not make it in, the Team Leader must arrange to pick up cards at their home beforehand.

May 1 – 6: Leadership Team and Board members complete **mop-up calls**.

May 6 (Saturday evening): Stewardship Drive Leadership Team receives **final reports** and all outstanding cards.

May 7: (Sunday morning): Celebration of results with the congregation. **Canvass over!**

May and June: Stewardship Drive **Chair prepares report** to the Board. Leadership Team members recruit the next year's Chair (perhaps from among their own).

Appendix 7
Giving Guide and Pledge Form

THE COMMUNITY CONGREGATION
STEWARDSHIP SUPPORT GUIDELINE

How you spend your money reflects what is important to you. When considering stewardship please think about what The Community Congregation has meant to you and your family, and how your involvement here continues to impact your life. Giving 5% or more of your net income says in clear terms that your church, the values it helps you to live by, and this community of friends all have a significant place in your heart and in your life. Use the table below as a guideline and please consider making this congregation your primary charitable beneficiary.

Monthly Net Income (more than)	Supporter % Support	Supporter Monthly Payment (minimum)	Sustainer % Support	Sustainer Monthly Payment (minimum)	Promoter % Support	Promoter Monthly Payment (minimum)	Visionary Tithe % Support	Visionary Tithe Monthly Payment (minimum)
$1,000	2.0%	$20	3.0%	$30	5.0%	$50	10.0%	$100
$2,000	2.0%	$40	3.0%	$60	5.0%	$100	10.0%	$200
$3,000	2.0%	$60	3.5%	$105	5.0%	$150	10.0%	$300
$4,000	2.5%	$100	3.5%	$140	5.0%	$200	10.0%	$400
$5,000	2.5%	$125	4.0%	$200	5.5%	$275	10.0%	$500
$6,000	3.0%	$180	4.5%	$270	6.0%	$360	10.0%	$600
$8,000	3.5%	$280	4.5%	$360	6.0%	$480	10.0%	$800
$12,000	3.5%	$420	5.0%	$600	6.5%	$780	10.0%	$1,200
$16,000	4.0%	$640	5.5%	$880	7.0%	$1,120	10.0%	$1,600

Just started coming to the church? Checking things out? We'd be honored if you would become a **Member Friend** and make recognizable financial contributions. Your routine practice of helping our active community carry out its programs is greatly appreciated. By making regular gifts, even though you may not be fully committed, you are recognized as establishing a beginning relationship with The Community Congregation. You will receive a free subscription to our semi-monthly newsletter, be welcomed at all our member events and classes, and may freely register your children for our religious education classes.

Have you found that this church is right for you and your family? Do you find you have been a regular worshiper or active participant in other activities for six months or more? Do you feel welcomed, and trusting of the friends you have found here? You will feel right at home and gain the privileges of serving in a governance role when you become a **Supporting Member**.

Have you been involved at TCC for five years or more? Our expectation is that Supporting Members consistently increase giving during the first three to five years of membership, eventually joining the circle of **Sustaining Members** of TCC.

Are you fully committed to liberal religion and the empowering message of Unitarian Universalism? Do you want to expand our services and our impact in Smithville? We joyfully welcome your personal journey as a **Promoter** or **Visionary**.

Yes! I (we) want to move this congregation forward!

I (We) will make gifts of $_____ each month to support The Community Congregation during the fiscal year ending June 30, 2010.

Please tell us whether you wish to make your stewardship payments _____Monthly (default) _____Quarterly _____Annually and, tell us if you would like information on how to use EFT to have your payments transferred from your bank account directly and routinely. We can set it up or we will help you work with your bank to do so.

Signed:_____ date:_____
Signed:_____ date_____

Sometimes unexpected events cause a change in priorities. If you find later on that you need to reduce or defer your stewardship commitment please let the Treasurer, Robin Greenbax, know. Thank you!

We would like to thank and recognize our most generous donors. **Recognition Levels will be displayed in the church lobby**. After considering the giving guidelines adopted by this congregation, please check the Recognition Level that applies to you:

_____ Basic Member or Friend (less than Supporting)
_____ Supporting Member or Friend
_____ Sustaining Member or Friend
_____ Promoting Member or Friend
_____ Visionary Member or Friend
_____ I (we) have checked one of the above Circles for statistical purposes but wish to be listed anonymously.

How to read the Stewardship Support Guideline –

Bob and Pam Jones retired on a monthly income of about $4,100. When they joined four years ago they made a commitment of $120/month so they would be Supporting Members and be able to vote on congregational issues. Pam Jones was recently elected a Trustee and Bob is active on the Building and Grounds Committee and teaches the middle school class. Pam and Bob have decided to increase their ongoing commitment from the current level of $145 to $200 because their income went up last year to nearly $5,000/month due to an inheritance, and they wish to be counted among the Sustaining Members – joining their good friends, Woody Burl and Daryl Ramirez.

Woody and Daryl have combined incomes of $18,500/month and have made a stewardship commitment of $900/month – even though Daryl has two daughters attending small private colleges. The two families have agreed on the desirability of becoming Promoters and have made a private pact to do so. Each will increase giving by 5 –10% per year for three years, reaching their goal after the Ramirez girls graduate.

Appendix 8
Canvasser Guidebook

The Community Congregation
CANVASSER GUIDELINES

Lawrence Lieder
Stewardship Drive Chair
123-4567
Your Stewardship Drive Team Leader is:

_____   _____

   Name   Phone

Your role as a canvasser is a critical element of a successful Stewardship Drive. You were asked to take on this responsibility because we trust your commitment to The Community Church. We have confidence in your desire to perform this function in an effective and timely manner. We appreciate your willingness to step forward in response to this request.

Please do not hesitate to call your Team Leader or me if you have difficulties or questions. The Stewardship Drive this year is critical to the healthy development of our church. Importantly, its success will depend in large part on whether our members feel that their own aspirations to find fulfillment will be met by the programs and opportunities afforded through our church. Let's work together to hear and respond to those callings. We are here to support you in the effort.

MAKING THE APPOINTMENT

You have two weeks to complete your calls. Make your appointments early. Give alternative specific times and ask which is better. (For Example, "I've got Wednesday and Thursday evenings open. Would one of those work better for you?") Usually they will choose one. If you ask "What would be a good time for you in the next two weeks?" they will more likely respond by scheduling in the second week or even on the last possible day.

A financial commitment is important in this stewardship drive. A conversation is equally important. We want you to spend time with members in a relaxed setting, like their home. Avoid canvassing at church or in the parking lot where there are distractions and interruptions.

Do not let the Commitment Card out of your control. Under no circumstances should you mail it out. The second best alternative is to fill it out for them based upon a phone conversation; you can then ask if you could drop by to get them to sign it. That's an opening to spend a few minutes in conversation.

There is an area on the Commitment Card for notes. Write down any information you gain when talking to them about TCC. Also keep notes on any attempts to contact them. This will be very helpful in coordinating your efforts as well as to us in the mop-up phase if you do not get through to them – for example, "4/27, 7:20, not home".

BEFORE THE CALL

Review the information card. It will usually indicate the names of the entire family, the number who are members of TCC, when they joined, whether children are in the religious education program, and the status of the current stewardship commitment. This will be helpful to have in mind as you discuss their involvement with TCC. *Note: This information is confidential and should not be discussed with others.*

Review the Vision Budget with the person(s) you will call on in mind. What are they most interested in? *Know the key items you will solicit their thoughts on.*

Before arriving, take a moment to center yourself on the challenge ahead of you. You are going to guide a discussion in which the person you are visiting will make an informed responsible decision in a non-judgmental atmosphere of trust and respect. The size of their pledge is not your responsibility. *You are responsible only for the integrity with which you facilitate this discussion.*

DURING THE CALL

Bring the following with you: Information and Stewardship Commitment cards
Preliminary Vision Budget
Questions and answers on pledging
Suggested Giving Table

Hand the person(s) the preliminary budget and allow them to look it over. You may have taken a highlighter to particular areas of the budget ahead of time. Call attention to those details. Find out what else is important to them for inclusion or expansion. Ask for permission to make a note of their comments or concerns.

Hand out a copy of the Giving Guide. Be prepared to discuss your own giving in general terms, such as identifying your support level. Ask the person which level they consider themselves. Be willing to discuss with them, if they wish, the basis for the Giving Guide.

Fill in the Stewardship Commitment card with them and have them sign and date it.

REPORTING BACK

We would like to have contact with you five times during the two week Stewardship Drive:

Sunday, April 15	Kick-Off lunch at Larry Lieder's. Pick up packets.
Wednesday, April 19	Telephone check-in with Team Leader
Saturday, April 22	Coffee and donuts. Turn in completed cards.
Wednesday, April 26	Telephone check-in with Team Leader
Sunday, April 29	Final canvasser meeting. Turn in remaining cards.

If you will miss one of the contact times or meetings, please call your Team Leader to provide an up-to-date report.

Appendix 9
Endowment Fund Policies

TCC ENDOWMENT FUND
STATEMENT OF GOVERNANCE

1)   The TCC Endowment Fund shall be under the general direction of the Board of Trustees, but shall be administered by an Endowment Committee consisting of five members, one of whom shall be the Senior Minister, *ex officio,* or his/her appointee. TCC Trustees shall appoint four other members of the congregation annually for one year terms beginning July 1, two of whom shall be current members of the Board. There shall be no limit to the number of terms an appointed member may serve.

2) The Endowment Committee shall work with the congregation to identify specific enduring programs worthy of endowed status. Each program shall be described as to its purpose, shall have a target funding level and date by which the congregation wishes to see the program launched. No program will be included in the Endowment Fund without the support of the congregation as expressed in a duly called congregational meeting.

3) The Endowment Fund shall be entirely isolated from the accounts of TCC. Further, there shall be no borrowing of endowment corpus, nor pledging of security. The TCC Endowment may be used only to further the objectives of endowed programs identified by the congregation.

4)   The Endowment Committee shall use the calendar year as fiscal year and shall report on its funds and programs at the annual meeting of the congregation.

5)   Income from endowment gifts shall be defined at the rate of the ten year Treasury bond on or about January 1 each year as applied to each endowed program's average quarterly assets of the prior three years. This calculation determines the income produced for the subsequent year in support of that program.

6) Until an identified enduring program has realized 75% of the endowed level targeted by the congregation, all income for that program shall be retained in the endowment and reinvested. Other program income shall be distributed to operating reserve accounts after the end of year reconciling calculation.

7)   Such other operational rules as the Endowment Committee shall find useful may be established, provided that they do not conflict with this Statement.

_____   _____

Secretary, Board of Trustees of TCC   date adopted

Appendix 10
Personnel Policies

THE COMMUNITY CHURCH

3000: PERSONNEL POLICIES

3010: Purpose. The intention of this congregation is to embody its Unitarian Universalist values and principles in its relationship to its employees. Toward that end these policies are intended to insure fair treatment of all employees, promote clearly understood responsibilities between employees and THE COMMUNITY CHURCH, and prescribe consistent and predictable personnel practices for all employees.

3070: Fiscal Responsibility. No supervisor shall authorize expenditures that will cause a budget program category to exceed the budget.

3071: No employee shall commit THE COMMUNITY CHURCH to spending that will cause total expenditures in a budget program category to exceed the budget.

3072: No employee shall be reimbursed for spending that will cause total expenditures in a budget program category to exceed the budget.

3080: Work Eligibility. All new staff members will be asked to fill out appropriate forms for payroll purposes and for personnel records. In accordance with the Immigration Reform Control Act of 1986 (IRCA), all new staff members at THE COMMUNITY CHURCH are also required as a condition of employment to provide documentation that establishes their identity and their legal right to work in the United States (Form I-9). Typically, this will happen prior to the first day on the job.

3090: Notification of Modification. The Board of Trustees may modify policies at any time. If any personnel policy changes, a copy of the change will be provided to each employee. Employees will be asked to sign a statement acknowledging reading, understanding, and accepting the terms and policies and any revisions to them.

3100: Discrimination and Harassment

3110: Non-Discrimination. TCC is dedicated to offering equal employment opportunity to everyone in calling, hiring, promoting, assigning and fully participating in the work of THE COMMUNITY CHURCH without regard to sex, age, disability, race, color, ethnicity, national origin, affectional preference, marital status, veteran or conscientious objector status, or religion (unless it conflicts with the Principles and Purposes of TCC).

3120: **Anti-Harassment.** Sexual harassment or harassment of any kind will not be tolerated by TCC, including harassment based on the above-named protected categories.

3130: **Remedy Process.** See Section 3800 for a description of the complaint process in the event of perceived discrimination or harassment.

3200: Types of Employment

3205: **Ministers** are generally Called by the congregation under terms agreed upon between the Minister and the Board of Trustees, in accordance with the bylaws of TCC. Non-Called Ministers may serve in special capacities by agreement with the Board of Trustees, in accordance with the bylaws of TCC. The general character of the ministerial employment relationship is consistent with these policies, but specific differences are governed by terms of the Ministerial Agreement entered into at the Call.

3210: **Salaried employees** are paid a predetermined annual salary commensurate with their position and do not receive overtime compensation. Salaried employment is characterized by positions that are not necessarily confined to specific hours, but tend to be defined by generalized expectations of a professional or non-routine nature.

3211: A salaried position involves responsibilities requiring one-quarter time or more.

3212: Usually salaried position responsibilities involve more interaction with the congregation, and are likely to require evening work such as attending committee meetings.

3213: Salaried employment is not characterized by keeping track of specific hours of work but rather by units of time required. (A unit is a morning, an afternoon, or an evening, and twelve units a week constitute full time.) The congregation will honor the general guideline that a one-quarter time salaried employee is expected to work three, and only three, units a week, although seasonal and other variations can and do occur.

3214: Salaried employees may work from a home office some of the time when approved by the supervisor.

3215: TCC encourages salaried employees to work as necessary without negatively affecting personal or family needs.

3220: **Regular Hourly** employment is characterized by a specific on-site work schedule.

3221: Regular Hourly employees are not expected to work from home.

3222: Regular Hourly employees may have routine contact with congregational members, but will not usually attend committee meetings as part of their duties.

3223: Regular Hourly employees are eligible to receive overtime pay.

3230: **Intermittent/Casual** employment is paid hourly, and either has no fixed schedule or is not dependant upon the same individual performing a scheduled task from one time to the next.

3231: Intermittent/Casual employees are frequently scheduled at the convenience of individuals in the group; as a consequence employment for any particular individual can be occasional and sporadic.

3233: Any work routinely scheduled for more than ten hours/week will not be staffed by Intermittent/Casual employees. Any employee working less than 200 hours/year is Intermittent/Casual. Positions budgeted or scheduled between 200 and 500 hours/year will be considered and classified by the Personnel Committee.

3240: **Contractual** employment involves work performed by individuals in circumstances only within the following guidelines.

3241: Contractors have wide latitude when and where work takes place. Duties routinely scheduled by THE COMMUNITY CHURCH are not likely to be contractual.

3242: A contractor has specified work objectives or outputs. There is little need for ongoing coordination or direct oversight of contractor work.

3243: A contractor is expected to provide supplies and materials. If THE COMMUNITY CHURCH provides supplies, tools, and workplace it is unlikely contractual employment.

3244: A contractor is likely to have a professional license or designation.

3245: A contractor operates an ongoing business with more than one customer or contract.

3246: TCC duties requiring quarter-time or more on an ongoing basis are not contractual.

3300: Wage and Salary Plan.

3310: **Intermittent/Casual Pay.** Intermittent/Casual employees will be paid a fair and equitable hourly rate, which will be more than the legal minimum wage. The rate will be adjusted as necessary, at least annually, for inflation and market conditions.

3311: Persons performing similar Intermittent/Casual duties will be paid equally. Some individuals are assigned oversight duties. They will be designated "Lead" and the hourly rate will be adjusted as appropriate.

3320: **Salaried and Regular Hourly Pay.** Each Salaried and Regular Hourly position will have a pay range established defining the lowest and highest acceptable wage for that job. The range will be set primarily in accordance with guidelines established by the UUA for similar congregations, modified for local employment market conditions if appropriate.

3321: The Personnel Committee is responsible for developing and maintaining factors and a protocol for establishing specific pay levels within a range, including consideration of experience, developmental training, and quality of performance.

3322: No employee will progress beyond the midpoint of a range based on experience alone.

3323: Any employee may be hired by TCC at a negotiated rate above the base rate. Such advanced placement will be based upon quantitative factors relating to education, training or prior experience. Decisions regarding quality of performance factors will be based solely in the TCC work environment over a minimum twelve month period.

3400: Leave

3405: **Application.** The conditions of paid leave set forth in this section apply to all Salaried and Regular Hourly employees, except that the Minister's Letter of Agreement contains separate provisions.

3410: **Unpaid Leave of Absence.** Occasionally employees face compelling personal needs that may require them to take time off from work.

3411: Unpaid leaves up to thirty days may be granted at the discretion of the supervisor, based on TCC's needs and the hardship that might result from their absence.

3412: Longer periods of leave require Board approval.

3413: Failure to return to work immediately following the granted leave of absence is regarded as a voluntary resignation.

3414: Regular Hourly employees will not be required by THE COMMUNITY CHURCH to take an unpaid leave of absence (for example, requiring two months of unpaid leave in the summer). Regular hourly employees are either working on their schedule or on a form of paid leave, unless they have requested and been approved for Leave Without Pay.

3420: **Funeral or Bereavement Leave.** Employees may be eligible for a leave of absence for up to one-half the normal weekly hours with pay for the death of an immediate family member. The scheduling of paid days off will be determined by the Supervisor or Business Manager based on the circumstances.

3430: **Jury Duty.** Employees called for jury duty are paid their regular pay as long as they are required to serve. Employees should appear for their normal schedule any day they are excused from jury duty.

3440: **Personal Leave.** Salaried and Regular Hourly employees have a leave plan designed to cover both planned vacation time and leave for an emergency, illness, or other life influences. (Such leave is referred to generically as "Personal Leave".) Personal Leave is divided between a Temporary Leave Account and a Permanent Leave Account, records of which are to be maintained by the Bookkeeper.

3441: Beginning immediately on hiring employees shall earn Personal Leave at the rate of one hour for every 20 paid hours. (This is about two and one-half weeks of leave annually.) Beginning with the employee's six year hiring anniversary Personal Leave will be earned at the rate of one hour for every 10 paid hours. (This amounts to about five weeks leave annually for full time employees.)

3442: Salaried employees will earn Personal Leave at the standard imputed rate: One-quarter time means 10 paid hours per week.

3443: Personal Leave is credited initially to a Temporary Leave Account. At the end of each fiscal year (June 30) the employee may direct unused Temporary Leave into a Permanent Leave Account, in an amount not to exceed the number of hours in their standard work week.

3444: The purpose of the Permanent Account is to provide employees an opportunity to build up an emergency leave account in case of extended illness or similar need, although its use is not limited by such circumstances. The balance in the Permanent Account will remain available until the employee uses it or terminates employment, at which time the balance will be paid out in full at the employee's then current wage rate.

3445: The Temporary Leave Account shall be reduced if necessary (after the annual transfer) to holding no more than the amount of Leave earned in the prior year. This unused Temporary Leave more than twelve months old shall thereby lapse.

3446: Upon termination of employment for any reason one-half of the unused Temporary Leave Balance shall be transferred into the Permanent Account for payout. The remaining Temporary Leave shall lapse.

3447: Personal Leave will be credited and used in whole hour increments only. It is available for use as soon as it is credited.

3448: It is expected that use of Personal Leave normally will be arranged and approved at least one week in advance with the employee's supervisor. Any leave taken without prior arrangement of at least 72 hours shall be charged to the employee's Permanent Leave account first.

3449: Upon adoption of this policy each qualified employee may have Permanent and Temporary Leave Accounts established based upon an assessment by the Business Manager and the Personnel Committee of existing Personal Leave credits (within the general spirit of these guidelines).

3450: **Holidays.** Salaried and Regular Hourly employees receive the following paid holidays: New Year's Day, Memorial Day, Independence Day, Labor Day, Thanksgiving Day, Christmas Day, and the Employee's Birthday.

3451: Because employees work various numbers of hours per week and various days of the week, during any week with a holiday the employee should normally work 20% fewer hours yet get paid the full amount. Hourly employees should list on their time card the appropriate number of hours as "Holiday Pay".

3452: Employees are expected to adjust their schedule in a holiday week in order to have the official holiday free of work duties.

3600: Benefits.

3605: **Non-Fungible Benefits.** THE COMMUNITY CHURCH will offer certain employee benefit programs and policies as outlined below. The cost of such benefits will be borne by TCC only as indicated. If an employee chooses to not receive a benefit as offered, the cost associated is not transferable for an alternative benefit or salary adjustment.

3610: **Pension Plan.** The following employees will receive pension benefits.

3611: An Employee must have attained the 18th birthday.

3612: The employee must have been paid for at least 1,000 hours in the prior 12 months and be expected to continue.

3613: The employee must have attained the one year employment anniversary date.

3614: Qualified employees will be enrolled in the UU Organizations Pension Plan.

3630: **Health Insurance.** The congregation will offer assistance in paying for health insurance coverage for all salaried and regular hourly employees who are normally scheduled to work ten or more hours/week.

3631: The standard level of support for any qualifying employee shall be based upon TCC paying a percentage of the premium cost equal to the percentage of time budgeted for them in their standard workweek, to a maximum of 80%.

3632: The TCC support will be provided for the entire premium, whether coverage is for an individual or family.

3633: If an employee is covered under another policy (for example, a spousal policy), TCC will arrange to pay the same proportion of the costs, up to the amount of out of pocket expense. This will be accomplished by increasing the employee's salary or budgeted hourly rate by the same amount.

Employees may be asked to provide evidence of the current policy covering them and the costs involved.

3634: Such support will begin after the four month trial employment period. (See Policy 3840.)

3640: **Long Term Disability Insurance.** TCC will obtain Long Term Disability Insurance for salaried employees and add the cost of the insurance to the employee's W-2. This is done so any resulting benefit payment will come to the employee tax free.

3650: **Dental Insurance.** TCC will pay the cost of dental insurance under the UUA Plan for salaried employees.

3660: **Employer FICA.** The employer share of the FICA tax will be budgeted for all employees including the minister. Since a minister must pay such tax directly, the employer share of FICA will be added to the minister's salary as additional W-2 income.

3661: In no case will the employer share of FICA not be budgeted for the minister. If an adjustment must be made to the budget before taking it to the congregation, the minister's salary amount will be reduced, rather than the FICA.

3680: **Education and Professional Development.** THE COMMUNITY CHURCH supports employees who wish to enhance their professional development and job-related skills through external training programs and conferences. In addition, employees may be asked to attend such programs and conferences as a participant or presenter. If an employee is required by her or his supervisor to participate in a training event, participation, up to 8 hours per day, will count as work time. In other cases, how much, if any, training time will count as work time will be established by the supervisor in consultation with the employee prior to the event.

3681: For some salaried positions, money may be allocated to cover professional expenses including the cost of outside training and conferences.

3682: Although THE COMMUNITY CHURCH does not cover the cost of continuing education, it will attempt to accommodate continuing education through flexible scheduling.

3700: Compensated Time.

3705: **Workweek.** The TCC workweek begins on Sunday and ends on Saturday.

3708: Any employee paid by hourly rate shall receive two hours minimum pay any time they are scheduled or called in to work.

3710: **Time Cards.** All regular hourly and intermittent employees must complete a time card for each pay period in which they work. This assures appropriate compensation for hours worked and fulfills legal requirements. If more hours are recorded than an employee is regularly scheduled for, the employee's supervisor or the Business Manager must sign the time card.

3720: **Overtime.** Overtime work is that exceeding 40 during the week and is assigned because of conditions and circumstances which merit extra compensation.

3721: Overtime work is compensated at 1.5 times the regular rate of pay.

3722: The employee's supervisor or the Business Manager must approve overtime.

3730: **Compensatory Time.** "Compensatory time" (*a.k.a.* "comp time") is non-scheduled time or overtime worked for which the employee is granted future time away from the regular hourly schedule in lieu of pay.

3731: All applicable rules pertaining to overtime also apply to compensatory time.

3732: The supervisor has discretion over whether to grant overtime pay or compensatory time.

3733: Any compensatory time balance in excess of ten hours accrued by Regular Hourly employees will be paid out after 30 days. Salaried employees will lose any earned compensatory time balance after 30 days.

3734: Compensatory time, both earned and used, must be reported to the Business Manager who will maintain a record of all such transactions.

3800:   Complaints, Discipline, and Terminations.

3805: **Complaints.** As a matter of general policy, supervisors will provide an open door for discussion and a receptive ear and will review all staff member's suggestions or complaints concerning our work practices and procedures.

3806: If an employee feels that she or he is being harassed or illegally discriminated against by anyone in TCC, she or he should first make it clear to the person they feel is the source of the harassment that the behavior is unwelcome and inappropriate. If the harassment persists or is particularly egregious the employee should report it immediately to her or his supervisor, the Business Manager, the Minister, the Personnel Committee, or any member of the Board of Trustees.

3810: **Complaint Procedures.** If an employee wishes to make a formal complaint, it should be done within a reasonable time after the incident has occurred or the issue has arisen. We consider an open discussion between employee and supervisor as the first step in the complaint process.

3811: The supervisor must respond to the complaint in a timely manner, not to exceed two weeks.

3812: If the supervisor does not resolve the complaint within two weeks or if the staff member disagrees with the supervisor's solution, the staff member may appeal to the Board of Trustees. Such appeals must be in writing with the nature of the grievance clearly outlined. The Board will investigate the complaint and notify the staff member, in writing, of a decision within a reasonable amount of time.

3813: If an employee is accused of harassment, the accused will be given the opportunity to explain and present any evidence to the contrary. If an accusation is substantiated the accused will be disciplined as appropriate, which may include, but is not limited to, termination of employment, depending on the circumstances.

3814: If the claim is substantiated it is the Board's responsibility and intention to take measures to ensure a safe work environment. If the claim cannot be substantiated, the accused will be reminded of the policy and the situation will be monitored for a reasonable period of time to protect everyone involved.

3815: The resolution recommended by the Board will be binding upon the congregation and employee.

3816: Retaliation or reprisal against employees who report harassment claims is prohibited and will not be tolerated. Any violation of this policy will be treated as a serious matter and will result in disciplinary action, up to and including termination.

3817: Repeated false claims of harassment are disruptive to the business of TCC and may be grounds for disciplinary action, including dismissal.

3819: If the employee has any questions about this policy or wonders whether an event constitutes harassment, the employee should immediately contact her or his supervisor, the Business Manager, the Minister, any member of the Personnel Committee or the Board of Trustees.

3820: **Employee Discipline.** Actions by staff members that are inappropriate for the work environment, are a hindrance to effective job performance, or violate policy, constitute improper conduct and may be cause for disciplinary action. THE COMMUNITY CHURCH maintains a progressive and participatory disciplinary system, which may include the following steps:

3821: Documented oral warning.

3822: Written warning.

3823: Based on circumstances, suspension with pay.

3824: With Board approval, suspension without pay and/or termination of employment.

3825: Based on circumstances, a supervisor may choose disciplinary action at any step in the process, including immediate suspension and recommendation of dismissal.

3826: All disciplinary action beyond oral warning requires notification to the Personnel Committee and the Board of Trustees.

3827: The employee will be given the opportunity to submit a written response to any documented disciplinary actions. The employee's written response will be attached to the disciplinary documentation and included in the personnel file.

3830: **Termination.** A termination may be voluntary or involuntary.

3831: If an employee decides to resign from employment at THE COMMUNITY CHURCH, we ask that she or he give a minimum of two (2) weeks notice, submit a letter of resignation, and have an exit interview with the supervisor or Business Manager.

3832: An employee is considered to have resigned if the employee does not return from a leave of absence, or has an unexcused absence of three consecutive scheduled work days or of seven consecutive calendar days, whichever is shorter.

3833: The employee must return all Fellowship property, including keys, credit cards, computer equipment, passwords, and all documentation issued during the course of employment.

3834: THE COMMUNITY CHURCH reserves the right to terminate any employee at any time, with or without cause or notice. Involuntary termination requires action by the Board of Trustees, except during the trial employment period.

3840: **Trial Employment Period.** The first four months of employment constitutes a trial employment period. This introductory period for all employees is meant to provide the employee and THE COMMUNITY CHURCH with an opportunity to evaluate the working relationship.

3841: During the trial period, an employee's supervisor may terminate employment for any reason without prior approval of the Board of Trustees. In such a case, a report will be made to the Personnel Committee and the Board of Trustees.

3850: **Regular Employment Period.** After the trial employment period, employment may be terminated only by action of the Board of Trustees. Generally, an employee with poor work performance or problem behavior will be given the opportunity to improve prior to termination.

3860: **Job Elimination and Layoffs.** Cutbacks or staff restructuring may be deemed necessary. THE COMMUNITY CHURCH will strive to minimize the negative impact on current employees if a reduction in the workforce is planned. Should such a layoff be necessary, all affected staff members will be given as much advance notice as possible.

3900:   General Conditions of the Workplace.

3901:   TCC's property and equipment are for legitimate business use only.

3902:   When TCC provides Internet access (including e-mail) to its staff members, it is to assist and facilitate business communications and work related research. These services are for legitimate business use only in the course of assigned duties. All materials, information, and software created, transmitted, downloaded, or stored on TCC's computer system are the property of TCC and may be accessed only by authorized personnel.

3903:   Limited personal use of TCC's computers and internet access is allowed for employees to perform personal tasks (e.g. check personal email, do word processing tasks, etc.) subject to the following limitations:

  a) Personal use of the computer and access line must not interfere with regular church business. This includes tying up phone lines for long periods while accessing the ISP.

  b) Personal use of church property may not incur cost to TCC. Personal toll calls, for example, may not be made at church expense. An exception is allowed in the case of brief calls by employees on immediate family business.

  c) No personal data or files are to be stored on TCC computers.

3910: **Employees as Volunteers**. A volunteer is someone who donates time without expectation of compensation. Volunteer service at TCC on the part of staff members is never expected and is generally discouraged, in order to avoid confusion of roles. If an employee does volunteer, it is imperative that the line be clearly drawn as to when the employee is in her or his staff role and when she or he is a volunteer. Employees shall strictly avoid volunteering for activities, which closely resemble their paid work.

3911: Staff responsibilities must take priority over any volunteer or membership interest.

3912: Issues regarding other staff members shall be addressed through staff channels, rather than volunteer channels.

3920: **Counseling.** Paid staff members, even if members or supporting friends of THE COMMUNITY CHURCH, are not eligible for pastoral counseling with the Minister.

3930: **Reviews and Goal Setting.** Salaried and Regular Hourly employees will have an employment review at the end of the trial employment period and once a year thereafter.

3931: Each employee will set goals for the following year with her or his supervisor. Those goals will focus on positive development of the employee and the employee's progress and job needs.

3932: The annual review process will be cooperative and is designed to facilitate positive, constructive communication between employees and supervisors. The form for documenting performance reviews will include a place for the employee and supervisor to sign and date documenting that the employee has had an opportunity to read the evaluation before it is entered into the personnel file. In the event that an employee takes exception to the content of the evaluation, the employee may attach a written rebuttal to the evaluation and this *too* will be included in the personnel file.

3940: **Work Schedule, Flextime, and Off-Site Work.** Flextime is an approved deviation from an employee's regular work schedule. Off-site work is work performed at some location other than TCC. Regular work schedule and work location are to be arranged for optimal effectiveness, with the approval of the supervisor. The supervisor, on a case-by-case basis taking into account the needs of TCC and the needs of the employee, will decide approval of flextime or offsite work.

3945: There are generally no funds available for work beyond the budgeted amounts. Hours worked in addition to the regular schedule require authorization of the employee's supervisor.

3950: **Pay Periods.** Paychecks are produced weekly, providing time cards are received in a timely manner for processing. Checks will be available at TCC no later than ten days after the end of the pay period. Alternate pay schedules may be arranged by specific mutual agreement between the employee and the Treasurer.

3951: Salaried employees will be paid $1/52^{nd}$ of their annual salary each week.

3960: Minimum Wage. All employees except those providing custodial care of children will be paid at a rate at least as great as the minimum wage.

3970: **Attire and Personal Conduct.** THE COMMUNITY CHURCH reserves the right to define appropriate standards of appearance for the workplace. It is expected that employees will maintain a clean and neat appearance, in accordance with their position, and will project a professional and business-like image in dealing with other staff, members, visitors, and the general public.

3971: **Confidentiality.** Employees may have access to confidential information about the Employer, including, but not limited to information about members, friends, or other staff members. Such information must remain confidential and may not be released, removed from TCC's premises, copied, transmitted or in any other way used for any purpose by employees outside the scope of their employment. All requests for information concerning past or present employees received from organizations or individuals should be directed to the Business Manager.

3980: **Safety and Inspection Rights.** Employees are expected to employ safe work practices on the job and on the church property.

3981: Threats, threatening behavior, or acts of violence by anyone on church property will not be tolerated.

3982: Churches, like other organizations, are sometimes the victims of thieves. The church has on its premises storage facilities such as desks, file cabinets, closets and storage areas for the use of employees, however, the church can make no assurances that they will always be secure. The storage of any unauthorized alcohol, illegal drugs, or drug-related paraphernalia is prohibited on church premises. Therefore, THE COMMUNITY CHURCH reserves the right to open and inspect any desk, file cabinet, storage closet, or storage area at any time and without prior notice or consent. Employees may not use personal locks on church owned desks, cabinets, closets or storage areas.

3990: **Personnel File.** It is important that an employee's personnel file contains up-to-date information. Employees should advise their supervisor or the Business Manager immediately whenever there are changes in their personal data, such as address, telephone number, marital status, domestic partners, number of dependents, and person to notify in case of emergency.

3991: Employees have the right to inspect their personnel file during regular work hours, given reasonable notice to their supervisor or the Business Manager. Employees may obtain copies of any document contained in their personnel file to the extent required by law.

3992: Personnel records are the property of THE COMMUNITY CHURCH and are not allowed to be taken from the Business Manager's office without authorization.

3993 Employees may request that additional documentation be added to their personnel file. This may include letters of commendation, award certificates, documentation of training received, written rebuttals of unfavorable personnel evaluations, or employee's written response to disciplinary actions. See the subsections on "Reviews and Goal-Setting" and "Employee Discipline" for more guidance as relating to those specific personnel actions.

Appendix 11
Sample Wage Scales

Basic Eight-Step Compensation Scale
For Regular Hourly Employees
Currently Office Assistant, Sexton, RE Assistant, and Business Manager

Base	Less than 1 year of recognized experience.
1	Each year of satisfactory performance review. Maximum of four steps.
1	Additional step given for an excellent performance review (maximum of four steps). During the first four years it is possible to combine longevity and performance steps (maximum two per year).

Each salary range is broken into 9 steps, increasing in 8 equal increments from the Base. The Base, or Step 0, is the minimum salary in range; Step 8 is maximum salary in the range. Steps are accumulated based on years of experience and performance excellence. Steps, once assigned, remain with the employee for the duration of employment. No provision is made to "retract" a step once granted.

Notes:

1. When an employee is first hired consideration may be given for experience prior to The Community Congregation up to a maximum of 4 years. Experience in a prior position should take into consideration the degree of comparability in responsibility and duties.

2. Obtaining longevity steps represents the progression of an employee from novice to fully proficient by accumulating the knowledge and skills to perform one's responsibilities adequately. This progression is presumed to occur sufficiently with or without a performance evaluation. An annual performance evaluation may suggest areas where improvement is possible, or it may establish grounds for possible termination. But, only in very unusual circumstances will a longevity step be withheld pending improvement.

3. An employee may advance more quickly from Base to Step 4 by demonstrating excellent performance. Each year of excellent performance during the first four years accrues the employee 2 steps, one for longevity and one for quality performance.

4. Experience alone will garner a maximum of 4 steps. Advancing beyond Step 4, requires excellent performance during employment with the congregation.

5. In rating work performance, supervisors should consider the following performance factors: skillfulness in doing the work, quality of work relations (communication, demeanor, attitude), reliability (attendance, punctuality, follow-through on tasks), and dedication and initiative (doing more or better than the minimum required).

Advanced Eight-Step Compensation Scale
For Salaried Employees
Minister, Director of Religious Education, Music Director

Base	Less than 1 year recognized experience.
1	For each 2 years of experience (except 1 after the first year), maximum of 4 steps.
1	Advanced professional training or degree in a closely related field, maximum 2 steps
1	Exceptional leadership or service to the congregation, maximum 2 steps.
1	Exceptional leadership or service to the denomination, maximum 1 step.
1	Exceptional leadership or service to the broader community, maximum 1 step.

Each salary range is broken into 9 steps, increasing in 8 equal increments from the Base. The Base, or Step 0, is the minimum salary in range; Step 8 is maximum salary in the range. Steps are accumulated based on years of experience, advanced training, and performance excellence. Steps, once assigned, remain with the employee for the duration of employment. No provision is made to "retract" a step once it has been granted.

Notes:

1. Consideration may be given for prior work experience when an employee is first hired. Comparable experience will take into consideration required duties and degree of responsibility. A maximum of four steps may be awarded to any employee for experience, including those awarded upon hiring. That is, experience alone gets an employee only to mid-range.

2. An employee will advance one step after the first year of satisfactory performance and one for each two years beyond the first, provided no more than four in total are awarded for experience. Experience steps represent

de facto progression as the employee accumulates knowledge and skills to perform in a fully proficient manner.

3. Advanced professional training steps are gained from one or more years of relevant guided learning beyond the minimum educational qualification for the position. For a minister, for example, this could be a degree beyond Master of Divinity or credentialing in a specialty field such as counseling or community organizing. Such steps may be assigned at the start of employment if the candidate already possesses an advanced degree, credentials, or training or may be earned after employment begins.

4. Steps for Exceptional Leadership may be obtained at any time after employment of at least one year at The Community Congregation. These steps are granted when the employee goes beyond the basic requirements of the position and reaches out to the broader calling of the profession. A certain amount of leadership and innovation is part of the normal expectation of professional employment. Exceptional leadership or service means going significantly beyond the ordinary, however that is judged. Since it confers a permanent increase in compensation level, exceptional leadership or service must have corresponding duration or significance.

5. Because assigning "Exceptional Leadership" steps is a highly subjective determination, it will be based on a specific recommendation to the Board of Trustees by a committee assigned to evaluate that question. For the Minister, an ad hoc committee could be made up of representatives from the Committee on Ministry, Personnel Committee, and Board of Trustees. For the Director of Religious Education, a similar ad hoc committee including representatives from the Religious Education Committee, Personnel Committee, and Board of Trustees could be formed. The Board of Trustees should then take formal action to accept or reject the committee's recommendations within 60 days of receiving it.

6. Advanced training or Exceptional Leadership steps remain with the employee, adding to the steps obtained through length of service.

Examples:
1. A minister with no prior experience is Called at Base salary. After one year of acceptable service, she is placed at Step 1. Every two years she advances another step, until reaching the mid-step (Step 4) after seven years.

2. The Minister has served two years, a year at Base and one year at Step 1. The ad hoc evaluating committee and the Board determine that she has demonstrated Exceptional Leadership. She is advanced immediately to Step 2. After completing the third year of service she is advanced to Step 3 based on an accumulated experience step.

3. The Director of Religious Education is currently at Step 1. He completes a credentialing module requiring more than a year of study. He is advanced to Step 2.

4. The DRE was advanced to Step 2 a year ago. This next year he demonstrates Exceptional Leadership to the denomination by developing and publishing a new curriculum. At the recommendation of the ad hoc committee the Board assigns a step for Exceptional Leadership, plus he accumulates a step for the two additional years of service. He is advanced to Step 4, with only two of the steps resulting from experience.

Appendix 12
Recording Pay & Benefit Decisions

MINISTER   THOM KATZ
(salaried position)

		04/05	05/06	06/07	07/08	08/09	09/10
Start Date	8/1/1999						
Recognized longevity		8	9	10	11	12	13
FTE		1.00	1.00	1.00	1.00	1.00	1.00

RECOMMENDED FAIR COMP RANGE (includes inflation adj.)

	04/05	05/06	06/07	07/08	08/09	09/10
high end	$88,100	$89,700	$91,400	$92,844	$97,500	$100,000
base	$59,000	$59,600	$61,000	$61,000	$61,000	$62,300

PLACEMENT IN RANGE

	04/05	05/06	06/07	07/08	08/09	09/10
Longevity points	4	4	4	4	4	4
Work Quality Points	0	0	1	1	2	2
Prof. Devel. Points	0	1	1	1	1	1
TOTAL	4	5	6	6	7	7

SALARY (incl. housing)

	04/05	05/06	06/07	07/08	08/09	09/10
Target Fair Comp plus bonus	$73,550	$78,413	$83,800	$84,883	$92,938	$95,288
Catch-Up Rate		33%	50%	75%	100%	
Pers. Comm. Proposal	$50,000	$59,376	$70,900	$80,912	$92,938	$93,000
Budgeted Salary	**$50,000**	**$58,000**	**$69,000**	**$80,000**	**$93,000**	**$95,300**
Housing Allowance	20,000	20,000	20,000	25,000	25,000	25,000

TAXES

	04/05	05/06	06/07	07/08	08/09	09/10
Employer FICA	$3,100	$3,596	$5,279	$6,120	$7,115	$7,290
Medicare	$725	$841	$1,001	$1,160	$1,349	$1,382
Workers Comp.	$74	$86	$103	$119	$138	$142
TOTAL TAXES	$3,899	$4,523	$6,382	$7,399	$8,601	$8,814

BENEFITS

	04/05	05/06	06/07	07/08	08/09	09/10
% Retirement Contrib.	5%	5%	6%	8%	10%	10%
$ Retirement Contrib.	$0	$3,319	$4,698	$7,228	$10,167	$10,454
Health Ins.	$3,450	$3,600	$3,600	$3,750	$4,000	$4,000
Long Term Disability	$300	$348	$414	$480	$558	$953
TOTAL BENEFITS	$3,750	$7,267	$8,712	$11,458	$14,725	$15,407

	04/05	05/06	06/07	07/08	08/09	09/10
% Professional Expense Allow.	3%	3%	5%	6%	7%	7%
Professional Expense Budget	$1,500	$1,740	$3,450	$4,800	$6,510	$6,671

MINISTER'S W-2 INCOME

	05/06	06/07	07/08	08/09	09/10
Salary, incl. Housing Allow.	$58,000	$69,000	$80,000	$93,000	$95,300
plus, transfer of Employer FICA thru Minister	$4,437	$5,279	$6,120	$7,115	$7,290
plus, health insurance cost on spouse's policy	$3,600	$3,600	$3,750	$4,000	$4,000
plus, premiums for Disability Ins.	$348	$414	$480	$558	$953
less, Housing Allowance	$20,000	$20,000	$25,000	$25,000	$25,000
less, Salary deferrals into Retirement Plan				$3,000	$3,000
W-2 INCOME	**$46,385**	**$58,293**	**$65,350**	**$76,673**	**$79,543**

Payment in lieu of Employer FICA: The total social security tax is 15.3% and shared equally by employers and employees – each pays 7.65%. A minister is a self-employed person however, under IRS rules. Consequently a minister pays both the employer and the employee share of FICA. In order to present a clear picture to the congregation, identify the minister's salary in the budget without employer FICA. This makes the salary number comparable to what the rest of us know as salary. Budget employer FICA for all employees, including the minister, separately. Pay the portion for the minister (normally sent to the IRS) as an add-on to the minister's salary. The minister is then responsible for turning it in.

Some congregations refuse to pay the additional employer FICA to the minister. It is not clear to me why a congregation and minister would disagree on this item. The minister must pay the employer FICA anyway. If a congregation "cannot afford to pay FICA" it is not the FICA which is not paid. Rather, it is the real, after-tax ministerial salary which is reduced. The budget should reflect a lower salary as well as FICA for the minister. This gives an honest accounting of what the congregation is paying as salary without changing the budget total. Congregational leaders need to portray to parishioners a salary figure accurately computed on a basis comparable to what they themselves get. Otherwise don't call it salary; it is contract employment.

Disability Insurance is income replacement insurance in the event some disabling tragedy befalls a key and valued employee. It is expensive but very advantageous to the congregation since it allows for replacement ministry or service without as great a financial burden on the church members during a difficult period. Benefits are taxable income if the church has paid the premium. Therefore the employee should pay the premium so any benefits paid will be tax free. Simply add the premium to the employee's salary and let the individual pay for it directly. He or she then also pays income tax each year on the additional income. The church will want to assure, of course, that the policy is paid for.

Housing Allowance is sometimes misunderstood since it does not apply to laity as such. Housing allowance is simply an IRS rule for a minister or military officer which allows some of their income to come to them tax free. (Think of it as the God and Country exemption.) The amount of the Housing Allowance must be established by Board action prior to the beginning of the fiscal year in which it is paid. If the budget contains the housing allowance and is adopted prior to the fiscal year, this is sufficient. Some churches pay the housing allowance by separate check to keep it clear of W-2 income.

The minister has the burden of demonstrating to the IRS that the allowance was less than housing costs; if not, excess (unused) housing allowance is treated as additional taxable income. The housing allowance portion of salary need not be included as income reported on the W-2 form.

It could be like most other itemized deductions: included on the W-2 as income and then taken off later as a series of individual deductions – but it is not. Like many other parts of the tax code it can be thought of as strange or unfair or an historical oddity. Or, it can be thought of as a nice tax break ministers get. It is whatever it is. It is worth noting that most of us take some housing costs, like mortgage interest, as itemized deductions. That is the largest item most ministers deduct too in documenting housing allowance costs. So, laity are not excluded entirely from the effects of "housing allowance"— probably getting two-thirds of what most ministers claim.

Health Insurance: As an arbitrary guideline, congregations should expect to pay at least 80% of the health insurance premium for full time employees and 50% of the premium for other family members. It is good if congregations can pay more, given the potential for catastrophic results of staff families with uninsured health costs.

If an eligible employee is covered under a spousal plan, the congregation should verify the costs and increase the salary by a similar amount or put the money into a Health Savings Account for the out-of-pocket expenses of health care. Congregations that look to save money by taking advantage of spousal coverage will be hit with sticker shock when they need to hire a new employee.

OFFICE ASST.   HERB HANDY
(regular hourly position)

Start Date 4/22/2003	04/05	05/06	06/07	07/08	08/09	09/10
Recognized longevity	1	2	3	4	5	6
Budgeted Hours/Week	10	12	15	20	20	25

RECOMMENDED FAIR COMP RANGE (includes inflation adj.)

	04/05	05/06	06/07	07/08	08/09	09/10
high end	$12.21	$12.21	$12.55	$12.74	$13.17	$13.56
low end	$8.32	$8.56	$9.13	$9.13	$9.28	$9.78

PLACEMENT IN RANGE

	04/05	05/06	06/07	07/08	08/09	09/10
Longevity step	1	2	3	4	4	4
Work Quality Bonus Steps	0	0	0	1	1	2
TOTAL	1	2	3	5	5	6

HOURLY RATE

	04/05	05/06	06/07	07/08	08/09	09/10
Target Fair Comp plus bonus	$8.80	$9.47	$10.44	$11.39	$11.71	$12.61
Catch-Up Rate		33%	50%	75%	100%	
Personnel Comm. Proposal	$8.75	$9.00	$9.75	$11.00	$11.75	$12.60
Budgeted Rate	**$8.75**	**$9.00**	**$9.75**	**$10.75**	**$11.75**	**$12.60**
Budgeted Cost	**$4,550**	**$5,616**	**$7,605**	**$11,180**	**$12,220**	**$16,380**

TAXES

	04/05	05/06	06/07	07/08	08/09	09/10
FICA	282.10	348.19	581.78	855.27	934.83	1,253.07
Medicare	65.98	81.43	110.27	162.11	177.19	237.51
Workers Comp.	6.77	8.36	11.32	16.64	18.18	24.37
TOTAL TAXES	354.85	437.98	703.37	1,034.02	1,130.20	1,514.95

BENEFITS

	04/05	05/06	06/07	07/08	08/09	09/10
% Retirement Contrib.				8%	10%	10%
$ Retirement Contrib.				$894	$1,222	$1,638
Health Ins.				$3,700	$4,000	$6,180
Long Term Disability				$70	$77	$197
TOTAL BENEFITS				$4,664	$5,299	$8,015

Appendix 13
Chart of Accounts
(Presumes "modified cash" accounting standard.)

The Community Congregation
CHART OF ACCOUNTS

1000	**ASSETS**	
1100	**Cash and Current Assets**	
1110	petty cash	(includes petty cash receipts not yet entered on books)
1120	undeposited funds	(includes credit card transactions not settled)
1130	checking account	
1140	prepaid expenses	
1200	**Savings**	
1210	CD's	
1220	Investments	
1300	**Long Term Assets**	
1310	equipment	(only if depreciation is used)
1320	land	(at cost)
1330	building	(at cost; see discussion on depreciation)
2000	**LIABILITIES**	
2100	**Current Debt**	
2200	**Notes, Mortgage and Long Term Debt**	
2210	principal outstanding	
2220	principal amounts in reserve	
2230	principal amounts paid	
3000	**REVENUE**	
3100	**Sustaining Gifts from Members and Friends**	
3110	stewardship commitments	
3111	annual drive	
3112	prior year commitments recovered	
3113	new member & non-canvass commitments	
3114	pre-paid commitments	(expense to reserves)
3120	special designated gifts	(expense to reserve)
3130	Sunday collections and other unidentified gifts	
3131	Change the World funds	
3132	operating support	(includes gifts beyond recorded pledge)

3200 **Sales of Services & Fees**
3210   RE registration fee
3220   enrichment workshops & classes
3230   special events and fund-raisers
3231   Auction (net)
3232   Fair Trade Coffee (net)
3240   minister's service fees   (to   minister's   discretionary fund)
3250   misc. sales
3251   newsletter subscription
3252   sermon copies

3300 **Misc. Income**
3310   endowment
3320   interest and capital gains
3330   income from TCC Corporation
3340   UUA grant

3400 **Use of Reserve Funds**
3410   Budgeted Transfers
3420   Unbudgeted Use of Reserves

4000 **EXPENSES**
4100 **Designated Gifts Expensed to Reserves**

4200 **Worship and Faith Development**
4210O   perational Expenses   (incl. committees)
4220   Compensation   (salaries only)
4221   Director of Religious Education
4222   Religious Education Assistant
4223   Sunday teachers & child care
4224   Music Director
4225   Accompanist
4226   Shared Ministry Coord.
4230   Children and youth programs
4231   supplies, materials
4232   curricula
4240   Adult enrichment and workshops
4250   worship materials
4260   library acquisitions

4270	pulpit expenses
4280	music
4290	Use of reserves, designated gifts, reimbursed exp.
4300	**Organizational Development & Operational Support**
4310	Board and misc. expenses
4320	Compensation & Related
4321	Bookkeeper
4322	Business Manager
4323	Minister
4324	Ministerial Intern
4325	Secretary
4326	Sexton
4327	Benefits (for all staff as appropriate)
4328	Payroll taxes (for all staff)
4330	Leadership Training and Development
4331	General Assembly and District Delegate support
4332	Staff training and development
4333	Other
4340	Communications (includes postage, phone, internet, newsletter, advertising)
4350	Financial management
4351	canvass
4352	bank charges
4253	endowment expenses
4360	Supplies
4361	building maintenance
4362	office
4363	kitchen
4370	Repair & Replacement (expense to reserve in July)
4380	Interest Expense (mortgage and loan costs)
4390	Use of reserves, designated gifts, and reimbursed exp.
4400	**Membership Support & Pastoral Care**
4410	Operational Expenses (incl. committees)
4420	Compensation
4421	event child care
4422	New Member Assist.
4430	Sunday hospitality (includes nametags, coffee, notecards)
4440	New Member Classes

4450	Retreats and Fun Raisers
4460	Pastoral Support
4470	Use of reserves designated gifts, and reimbursed exp.

4500	**Community Presence and Denominational Mission**
4510	Operational Expenses (incl. committees)
4520	Compensation
4521	Community Minister
4522	Campus Ministry
4530	Assistance to Individuals
4540	Community Organizations
4541	AIDS House
4542	Interfaith Council
4550	Nation and World
4551	Transylvania congregation support
4552	UUSC
4553	UNESCO
4560	Denominational Support
4561	area council support
4562	district dues
4563	UUA Annual Program Fund
4570	Use of reserves, designated gifts, and reimbursed exp.

5000	**RESERVES & EQUITY**
5100	**Reserves - Future Funding**
5110	Contingent Financing Reserves
5111	Pre-paid Commitments
5112	Late Expense Holding Acct.
5113	Emergency/Contingency
5120	Make the World a Better Place
5121	Helping Hand Fund (Minister's Discretionary Fund)
5122	Support to Other Organizations
5130	Pulpit Reserves
5131	Minister's Sabbatical
5132	Future Search
5140	Capital Improvement Savings
5141	Landscaping
5142	Aesthetics & Liturgical Art
5143	Repair & Replacement

5150	Religious Education
5151	YRUU Savings
5152	RE Program Development
5153	RE Social Action
5160	Note and Mortgage Reserves
5170	Leadership Development
5180	Music
5200	**Equity**
5210	Accumulated Savings - Prior Years
5220	Net of Current Operations

Appendix 14
Accounting

A FEW SIMPLE ACCOUNTING TRANSACTIONS

With the *Balance Sheet* (or *Statement of Financial Position*) and an *Income Statement* (or *Statement of Current Activity*) described in the section entitled "Right Brain Accounting," we established the general structure within which we can keep track of our financial affairs. Now let's look at a few transactions to get a clear picture of how it happens.

To begin, we'll imagine that the congregational members launch a campaign to raise $100,000 for a remodel in the religious education building. The church borrows money from its membership. The money all comes in during one generous weekend. On Monday morning, the church bookkeeper makes the following entries on the books:

INCOME STATEMENT		
	budget	actual
Revenues		
Expenses		
Net Surplus		unchanged

Assets and Liabilities increase, but there is no impact on the budget.

BALANCE SHEET	
Assets	
cash	+100,000
Total, Assets	
Liabilities	
building notes	+100,000
Reserves	
Accumulate Surplusses	
prior	
current net	unchanged
Total, Liabilities, Reserves, & Surpluses	

On Monday afternoon, a crew comes and erects a pre-fab building addition. The contractor is paid that evening. On Tuesday morning the bookkeeper makes the following entries.

BALANCE SHEET	
Assets	
cash	-100,000
building	+100,000
Total, Assets	unchanged
Liabilities	
Reserves	
Accumulated Surpluses	
prior	
current net	
Total, Liabilities, Reserves, & Surpluses	unchanged

Notice that nothing that has happened in these transactions has yet affected the Income Statement of the church. You will recall that all the operational activities of the congregation show up as changes on the Income Statement; that is, they show up as affecting the budgeted operations and are thus translated to the Current Surplus. Since we entered these transactions without changing the Current Surplus, we know we did nothing to affect the budget. Some people loaned the church money; it was borrowed and is not income. Then, the cash was changed into a building addition; the character of a church asset has changed but no money has been spent. These two transactions took place entirely on the balance sheet – no income, no spending.[18]

During the next year there are three items related to this building remodel however which are included in the budget: interest expense on the mortgage, principal reduction on the mortgage, and an expense for the building.

First, the notes used to finance the building will be paid in a lump sum in eight years, both principle and interest. The budget includes an annual interest expense of $6,500 (or $1,625 per quarter). Each quarter money is set aside in a reserve account as shown below. Notice that the expense is offset by an increase in reserves. The amount of cash available in the checking account is unchanged by this transaction; however some of that cash is now reserved.

---

18 I have made this perhaps simpler than I should; I ask that you imagine a contractor coming onto the church property and waving a magic wand over a pile of money, turning it into a building. From an accounting perspective this is all that has happened.

INCOME STATEMENT		
	budget	actual
Revenues		
Expenses		
interest on notes		1,625
Net Surplus		-1,625

BALANCE SHEET	
Assets	
Total, Assets	unchanged
Liabilities	
Reserves	
building note savings	+1,625
Accumulated Surpluses	
prior	
current net	-1,625
Total, Liabilities, Reserves, & Surpluses unchanged	

The amount set aside for principal repayment ($9,500 annually or $2,375 quarterly) is not an expense however. It was included in the budget because the congregation must come up with the cash to pay off the loan. But just as the original borrowing of funds was not "revenue" to the church, so too when we pay back principal on the mortgage notes this transaction is not an "expense" either. (When you make a payment on your own mortgage, you are reducing your mortgage balance somewhat. Many people do not think of that as '"spending" but as "forced saving".

The principal payments are handled as follows:

BALANCE SHEET	
Assets	
Total, Assets	unchanged
Liabilities	
mortgage	100,000
less principal in reserve	-2,375
Reserves	
mortgage reserve	+2,375
Accumulated Surpluses	
prior	
current net	
Total, Liabilities, Reserves, & Surpluses	unchanged

In these transactions, we borrowed money and paid the contractor. We paid interest on the loans into the reserve escrow account, and we set aside additional money in reserve to pay off the principal of the loans. What about the building itself?

The purpose of "depreciation" is to recognize the actual cost of a building as an expense to the organization that built it. A depreciation schedule spreads that cost, appropriately, over a number of years as the building is used, matching the cost of the building to the income stream occurring during "useful life" of the building. Because churches are not concerned with calculating "net profits" from that income stream however nor with determining annual tax liabilities, "depreciation" is a cost concept easily set aside by church leadership. It is forgotten in the press of immediate uses for cash. After years of neglect, the concept becomes distrusted.

The Finance Committee at The Community Church decided to use the general notion of depreciation, but to refer to it instead as "repair & replacement reserves." They will set aside 4% of the value of the building addition ($4,000) each year in reserves.

During the first quarter the bookkeeper makes the following entry.

INCOME STATEMENT		
	budget	actual
Revenues		
Expenses		
Repair and Replacement transfer		1,000
Net Surplus		-1,000

BALANCE SHEET	
Assets	
Total, Assets	unchanged
Liabilities	
Reserves	
Repair & Replacement Reserve	+1,000
Accumulated Surpluses	
prior	
current net	-1,000
Total, Liabilities, Reserves, & Surpluses	unchanged

Over time cash accumulates in the reserve accounts because of this expense.[19] Annual giving supports all the expenses, including the "repair & replacement reserves" item. When this expense is entered on the books, no money leaves the checking account. After 25 years, the congregation has not only an old, used but remodeled, building, but also $100,000 in savings in reserve with which to make the major repairs which will be required.

Gifts for Special Purposes

Another common problem is the handling of income and gifts intended for a specific purpose, particularly when no one is certain when the spending for that purpose will occur. Examples of such gifts might be the proceeds from a special Sunday offering earmarked for assistance to the partner church in Transylvania, or a car wash put on by the youth group. The question we face at such times is how

---

19   Nothing is done to change the value of the building on the balance sheet. This is not an acceptable accounting practice for most accountants. The rationale for not reducing the value of the building is that it is easier to continue to get the membership to understand the need for a 4% reserve expense each year if the building is shown as having substantial value. I would be loath to take the value of every church building in the denomination greater than 25 years of age to zero, fearing we would then lose the basis for further savings.

do we prevent such funds from getting "lost" in the general accounts of the church while holding them for (perhaps) an extended period of time?

My preference is to treat such an item as a special reserved amount until it is used, and the purpose of the gift has been accomplished. Such gifts are "revenue" but are immediately expensed to a reserve account until such time as they will actually be used.

Let's use the car wash example to see how this is done. The youth group conducts a hugely successful car wash and raises $1,000. The money will be partially used ($600) to support three members of the group in attending Leadership School next summer. The rest will be split between buying books for the youth library and supporting a local runaway teen shelter. Initially the entire $1,000 is put into reserves. This involves two transactions. First the revenue comes in and increases the church income. On the Balance Sheet cash increases.

INCOME STATEMENT	
budget	actual
Revenues	
YRUU Car Wash	1,000
Expenses	
Net Surplus	+1,000

BALANCE SHEET	
Assets	
cash	+1,000
Total, Assets	
Liabilities	
Reserves	
Accumulated Surpluses	
prior	
current net	+1,000
Total, Liabilities, Reserves, & Surpluses	

Then, an expense is entered as the money is credited to the reserve account. The income and expense have been offset so there is no budget impact. Cash has increased; and the reserve account is increased.

INCOME STATEMENT		
	budget	actual
Revenues		
Expenses		
Unbudgeted xfer to Reserves		1,000
Net Surplus		- 1,000

BALANCE SHEET	
Assets	
Total, Assets	
Liabilities	
Reserves	
YRUU Reserve	+1,000
Accumulated Surpluses	
prior	
current net	-1,000
Total, Liabilities, Reserves, & Surpluses	

The needed books are purchased the following weekend. The bookkeeper reimburses the group leader for them. Two transactions are entered. First, an amount equal to the expense is brought out of the reserve account and recognized as revenue to the church. Second, the expense is entered and a check is issued, reducing the checkbook balance.

INCOME STATEMENT		
budget		actual
Revenues		
Unbudgeted xfer from Reserves		119.50
Expenses		
Net Surplus		+119.50

BALANCE SHEET	
Assets	
Total, Assets	
Liabilities	
Reserves	
Youth Reserves	-119.50
Accumulated Surpluses	
prior	
current net	+119.50
Total, Liabilities, Reserves, & Surpluses	

INCOME STATEMENT		
budget		actual
Revenues		
Expenses		
Library Books		119.50
Net Surplus		- 119.50

BALANCE SHEET	
Assets	
checking account	-119.50
Total, Assets	
Liabilities	
Reserves	
Accumulated Surpluses	
prior	
current net	-119.50
Total, Liabilities, Reserves, & Surpluses	

The reserves cover the expense, so after both entries are completed on the books, the church income statement is again unaffected; neither the reserves nor the expense require any particular explanation to the Board. The remainder of the youth group car wash money is still reserved for later use. The bookkeeper is then asked to send off the money to Leadership School to secure a reservation. A similar set of transactions are entered.

INCOME STATEMENT		
budget		actual
Revenues		
Unbudgeted xfer from reserves		150.00
Expenses		
Net Surplus		+150.00

BALANCE SHEET	
Assets	
Total, Assets	unchanged
Liabilities	
Reserves	
Unbudgeted Use of Reserves	-150.00
Accumulated Surpluses	
prior	
current net	+150.00
Total, Liabilities, Reserves, & Surpluses unchanged	

INCOME STATEMENT		
budget		actual
Revenues		
Expenses		
Deposit for Youth Training		150.00
Net Surplus		- 150.00

BALANCE SHEET	
Assets	
checking account	-150.00
Total, Assets	
Liabilities	
Reserves	
Accumulated Surpluses	
prior	
current net	-150.00
Total, Liabilities, Reserves, & Surpluses	

Notice that it is possible to keep a clear record of special reserve amounts, and to retrace precisely what they have been spent on. This is true even though the reserve funds are intermingled with the accounts of the church. If anyone wants to know specifically how the $1,000 has been used, they can look at the entries in the reserve account and see when the $1,000 came in, and when and why each withdrawal was made from that account.

On the other hand, they also know the total amount spent on training by the church since both the youth group training expense and all other training expenses are included in the church books as part of total training costs for the church for that year. This method of accounting for special reserves tells the Board the true annual cost of running the church, including the use of specially raised gifts.

By the way, if you use this method for your congregation you will also need to be clear with the Board and the membership that the "adopted budget" gets routinely increased by spending of reserve amounts. This is because the use of reserves is often not budgeted — for example, the use of youth car wash funds we just saw. We did, however, increase both the revenue and expenses of the church with these funds. Such adjustments to the adopted budget should not require review and approval by the Board. The approval occurred when the Board said at some point that the youth group could have a car wash and raise money to support their program. Ostensibly the Board would also have said at the same time what the general parameters were for use of the money, or would have outlined purposes it in creating the reserve account as well as indicating who could approve specific uses.

Appendix 15
Accounting Understandings

IT'S THE LITTLE THINGS

There are many small, niggling problems in church accounting that can create confusion in the financial records unless they are handled similarly every time they come up over the years. There may not be a clear way to deal with particular problems. There may be differences of opinion. But, while such problems can legitimately be handled in any number of ways it is better for all to abide by a single way.

I suggest writing the preferred procedures down and keeping them in a binder that can be passed along from one treasurer to the next. Thus, there will be reasonably compatible budgeting and reporting from year to year.

It is not necessary that every treasurer absolutely must, without further thought, do things the way all predecessors did them. But by writing these issues down future treasurers will have an understanding of what has been done in the past and why.

Here are a few examples. None of these must be followed as set forth here.

ACCOUNTING UNDERSTANDING #1
PRE-PAID STEWARDSHP COMMITMENTS

Situation: Some stewardship commitments are paid in a lump sum prior to the beginning of the fiscal year for which they are intended. For example, at the time a person is visited they agree to give so much to support the congregation for the following year and write out a check for the amount at the same time.

Treatment: Such payments are to be brought immediately onto the books as a gift from the donor and an increase in cash. Then they are immediately expensed into the pre-paid commitment sub-account within the reserve contingency fund.

As soon as practical after the start of the fiscal year (certainly before the end of the first quarter) such reserves are to be credited as income from the reserve account. They are not treated as a donor gift at that time (since that already occurred). The crediting of all such payments is a single transaction, not spread throughout the year (since the cash has already been received).

The level of annual stewardship income expected each month should reflect all early payments as received in the first quarter.

Result: At year end there will nearly always be pre-paid stewardship gifts in reserve. By the end of the first month or so usually there will be none. It is conceivable, though unlikely, that someone might pre-pay their commitments a few years in advance in which case the reserve account would have a continuing balance.

K. Peter Henrickson
Finance Director

ACCOUNTING UNDERSTANDING #2
CREATING RESERVE ACCOUNTS

Situation: Someone or some group wants to contribute money for some particular future use. There is a strong feeling that the money needs to be "kept track of separately, in a separate account".

Treatment: Reserve accounts are used sparingly to avoid duplication, misunderstanding, and excessively cluttered financial statements. They are established by the Board in consultation with the Finance Committee. There will always be a written description of the intended eventual use of the account as well as a clear designation of who is recognized to authorize spending of the reserve amounts.

Reserve accounts are not used to isolate funds by source; rather, to isolate funds by purpose.

Result: There will be a smaller number of separate funds, and some of them will be used for multiple gift sources. Since the use for a single general purpose – for example, playground equipment – they can be co-mingled. A review of the ledger sheet for any reserve account will detail each separate gift and identify its source.

Peter Henrickson
Finance Director

ACCOUNTING UNDERSTANDING #3
TREATMENT OF DESIGNATED GIFTS AND RESERVES

Situation: Funds are given with a designation for some particular purpose. There is little predictability as to when such gifts will be received or spent.

Treatment: The receipt of funds for specific designated purposes is credited to income as "Special Designated Gifts". In general such gifts should be immediately expensed to one of the Future Spending Reserve accounts through "Transfers to Reserves – Special Gifts". (Even if it is clear the money will be used in the current fiscal year is best transferred to the reserve account so there is one place detailing all the transactions for that purpose.)

Usually funds coming out of Reserve accounts are not for anticipated and budgeted items. But, since spending reserves is directed by the appropriate person or committee it is certainly an approved expense of the congregation and requires a clear accounting of its use but no further authorization. The amount should be brought in as revenue, "Unbudgeted Use of Reserves". The expense should be incurred in the appropriate program area under "Unbudgeted Expenses from Reserves".

All entries in and out of reserve accounts should include a memo note explaining the transaction. Thus, a full accounting of any reserve account is available by reviewing the reserve account ledger, and of all incoming designated gifts by reviewing the Special Designated Gifts ledger.

Result: By using the above guidelines the budget will be unaffected by the receipt and use of special designated gifts while providing an accurate statements for the full financial operation of the church through the year.

K. Peter Henrickson
Finance Director

ACCOUNTING UNDERSTANDING #4
LATE EXPENSES

Situation: After the closing and reporting of a fiscal year there may be additional late expenses which come in for payment. These can upset the current year budget if they are large, creating an unplanned and unwarranted deficit situation.

Treatment: If such items are small (less than $200) they should be absorbed by the current year budget. Only if they are large, or in total are more than $2,000, should all or some be charged to the Emergency/Contingency Fund.

In the event they are specifically anticipated, the bookkeeper may expense unused budget line items for late expenses into the contingency fund before closing out the year. Such expenses occur on the line item that would ordinarily be used for the expense. Any such late expense reserves should not be on the books beyond the first quarter of the following year. Funds remaining in the Late Expense sub-account on October 1 will usually be brought into the current budget as "Use of Reserves" income.

Result: Once the books on the year are closed, the amount showing as Accumulated Equity will remain unchanged until the close of the following year. In rare circumstances that number may change mid-year if the Board transfers funds between Accumulated Equity and Reserves. Such exchanges occur only with the explicit approval of the Board.

K. Peter Henrickson
Finance Director

ACCOUNTING UNDERSTANDING #5
UNREIMBURSED EXPENSES

Situation: Someone donates supplies or some other item and does not seek reimbursement. The item is intended as a gift.

Treatment: Since such gifts are supportive of the operations of the congregation, one might believe that they should be reported and accounted for. If not, the financial statements do not reflect accurately the "true cost" of running the congregation.

In order to support such a stand however one must believe that three conditions will be met. 1) The gifts of supplies, snacks, and so on must be a material factor in the operation of that program. 2) All, or nearly all, of such gifts must be accounted for. And 3), the gifts are necessary to the program and vary greatly in level from year to year, creating unplanned expense levels. If any of these prove to not hold as true, the argument for pursuing an accounting for such gifts is considerably less robust.

Further, in that posture those who manage budgets in various areas of church administration must necessarily accept that gifts in kind will show up on their financial statements as expenses against their budget even though the items were donated. It is difficult to accept the notion that when someone donates supplies it is still an expense and actually reduces the remaining budget availability. However, the flip side of accounting for the "true cost" of an operation is that such items are reported both as income and expense.

For all these reasons: lack of materiality, lack of any control or knowledge about the "actual" extent of such gifts, and misunderstandings about how such gifts are to be accounted for, gifts in kind will not be routinely recorded onto the books.

Result: There may be occasions when this Accounting Understanding will be set aside, and some gifts in-kind will be accounted for, but most of the time such items will not be run through the books. It is still important to recognize and be appreciative of such gifts. And a written acknowledgment of such a gift can and should be given without entering a transaction in the financial records.

K. Peter Henrickson
Finance Director

Appendix 16
Mortgages and Loans

BALLOON PAYMENT LOANS

Most churches take on debt at some point. If it is a standard mortgage, it is clear how much is due each month and the board can plan payments in the budget. Sometimes a loan does not require current payments however. Sometimes loans are extended on the basis that a balloon payment will be made in the future. In such cases misunderstandings or disagreements can arise over the rate of saving which needs to occur to satisfy the loan in the future.

Suppose, for example, that a church borrows $10,000 from each of ten members with both interest and principal to be paid in a lump sum in the future. In particular, suppose that half of the loans are to be repaid with 5% annual interest in five years; the other half are to be repaid with 8% annual interest in ten years. No payments to the lenders are to be made until then. The following table sets forth one schedule under which reserves for these two notes could be accumulated.

Community Church
Mortgage Repayment Fund

	2003	2004	2005	2006	2007	2008	2009	2010	2011	2012
NOTE 1										
interest due	2,500	2,625	2,756	2,894	3,039					
principal due					50,000					
NOTE 2										
interest due	4,000	4,320	4,667	5,039	5,442	5,877	6,347	6,855	7,404	7,996
principal due										50,000
Annual Payment to Fund										
interest	6,500	6,945	7,422	7,933	8,481	5,877	6,347	6,855	7,404	7,996
principal	3,500	6,055	8,578	10,067	9,519	13,123	12,653	12,905	12,596	11,004
total payment	10,000	13,000	16,000	18,000	18,000	19,000	19,000	19,760	20,000	19,000
Funds Paid Out					63,814					107,946
Fund Balance	10,000	23,000	39,000	57,000	11,186	30,186	49,186	68,946	88,946	0

Notice that the principal and interest amounts are fixed by the terms of the notes. The "cash due" is simply the total interest and principal which must be on hand at each due date. The rate of savings is highly variable however. It depends on how much the congregation is able to add in the annual budget. It may also be influenced by a few generous gifts, the timing of which is uncertain. By setting forth the reserve requirement schedule in this format however, it is relatively easy to focus on annual requirements several years into the future and modify them, of course, as conditions change. Each year the finance committee can review the current status of the reserve savings, change the applicable interest rate if necessary, and determine savings to budget for the upcoming year.

Appendix 17
Auditing

"AUDITING" IN CHURCHES

Most churches don't audit the financial records, even every few years. A church is fairly small compared to corporate or business entities, making a professional audit a disproportionately large expense in a church budget. (Read on to see many of the steps involved in a well-done audit. An audit involves a great deal of professional time and is not cheap.) Against that, there always seem to be unfinished and more important things requiring our scarce resources. Further, it is not often that a church needs to have audited financial records to show to a bank or lender – it happens, but not often. Finally, it is easy and comfortable to think that in churches, of all places, an audit is not really very important. Even talking about an audit seems to entail questioning of the integrity of those who are responsible for the financial affairs of the congregation.

At the same time, it is that very attitude which makes churches such easy targets for fraud and theft. In the abstract most church leaders believe some kind of regular, periodic financial review by "independent people" ought to be done. It may even be a requirement of the bylaws (giving evidence to the frequent observation that Board members find it enjoyable adopting policy – its implementation that is a problem). Let's admit from the start that we are probably not going to change. We still want to be careful and responsible however; we don't want to pay simply to assure ourselves that we have been. We won't have a routine annual audit by a CPA. That doesn't mean however that we cannot have some level of care exercised in reviewing the church financial records and procedures. But, let's not maintain confusion regarding our solution by calling it an "audit". We can conduct a low level non-professional check-up instead of an audit.

What follows are ideas about how to go about such a check-up. (From here on I will refer to a "check-up" and to "checkers" rather than to an "audit" and "auditors" in an effort to make it clear this is not equivalent to a formal audit program.) This list of activities can be used by a team of laity to ensure that the asset protection, bookkeeping and financial reporting needs of their congregation are being carried out in a methodical and reliable manner. [20]

The Bylaws: Begin by noting what your bylaws might say: "There shall be a three member Financial Review Committee appointed by the Board and including

---

20 I am indebted to Larry Ladd who was the long time Financial Advisor to the Board of the Unitarian Universalist Association as well as Victoria Vincent, a correspondent on the UU-Money list serve, for the ideas presented here. Be assured that having a Financial Review Committee go through this list of activities does not preclude the importance of having a professional audit sometimes, particularly if there are serious questions about the veracity of the financial records.

at least one Board member. No member of the Finance Committee, or the Stewardship Committee, or church staff or contract employees may serve on the Financial Review Committee. The financial records of the congregation will be reviewed by the Committee following the close of the year with a report to the Board prior to the end of the first quarter. In addition such other review of records the Committee might find expedient during the rest of the year is expected."

Scheduling: There should be a regular time for conducting the check-up. In addition, there could be unannounced and somewhat random reviewing of various documents throughout the year. You can determine for yourself which of the items below might be interesting to look at mid-year.

Focus of the Check-Up: Many congregations do not maintain financial statements such as the samples in Appendix 2. Frequently the only record is one reporting on revenue and expenses versus what was budgeted. If that is the only financial statement prepared in your church, the records are not professionally auditable. Even though we said we are not doing an audit, it should be of some concern to you if your congregation could not even get an audit if you wanted one. If you do not have financial reports including what you own and what you owe, in addition to what you receive and pay out, the steps below are pointless. You should be worried.

Record order and retention: Even a church is required to have particular documents on file which establish the legal entity and its compliance with state and local laws. These documents should be maintained systematically and easily retrievable. The following list provides examples; use it to think about other possibilities. There may be other documents required in your community.

A. Where are current financial and personnel records kept? How long are the records being kept? Is there a policy or standard to comply with? Who is in charge of record retention?

B. Annual filing with the Secretary of State. Once you have begun to file, a reminder is usually sent from the state. The purpose of the filing is to maintain corporate status which in turn protects the board from some personal liabilities. If a corporation becomes legally "inactive" because this report has not been filed board members may be personally liable for a judgment.

C. Annual property tax exemption filed with the County. Failure to file could lead to a tax bill for the church, and subsequently could result in a tax sale of the property.

D. In the Unitarian Universalist denomination there is an annual report to the denomination in January. The filing of the report establishes official membership levels of the congregation. That number in turn determines the dues level and the number of delegates the congregation is entitled to at General Assembly and District meetings. The UUA bylaws state that anyone who is entitled to vote on congregational business is a member of the congregation for denominational purposes.

E. Copies of W-2 and W-4 forms issued to employees should be on file. Copies of quarterly reporting (941s) should also be on file. Check to see that the reported numbers match those on the financial statements and payroll reports, that reports are signed, dated, and sent on time.

F. IRS 1099 (Miscellaneous Income). The IRS requires that a 1099 be issued to all independent contractors and non-incorporated service providers paid more than $600 in a calendar year. With the 1099 the church should have a W-9 for each such contractor. If the identifying number on the W-9 is a personal social security number, the payment is to be made to the individual. If the number on the W-9 is an employer identification number, a 1099 is issued only if the service provider is unincorporated.

G. Form I-9. The employment eligibility verification plus supporting documentation should be on file for every employee.

H. Additional forms are required by various states when a new employee is hired. Make sure that all such forms are also on file.

I. Sales tax-exempt status letter from the state Department of Revenue should be on file. It must be renewed periodically. This requirement varies from state to state.

J. Historians want to keep board and congregational meeting minutes forever, and that is arguably a good objective. From the standpoint of managing the life of the congregation, orderly files of these should be readily accessible for ten years.

K. Look at the bank's list of authorized check signers. Is this a list of the appropriate people?

L. If payments of Unrelated Business Income Tax have been made, assure copies of the returns are kept for at least five years. Have all the returns been filed and the tax paid?

M. Review the church inventory of equipment or other attractive assets. Spot check that items on the inventory are still in the building. Note new additions to the inventory for the past year. Spot check that they have been properly marked with an inventory tagging system.

Computer records safeguards:

A. Are important records on the church computer backed up on a regular basis? Are backup files stored off-site?

B. Are the church offices locked when not in use? Is the computer locked or password protected? Is there adequate software safeguarding against on-line intrusion?

Are all expenses authorized and then paid timely? Various payments are critical to the financial and legal health of the congregation. Critical attention should be paid to the payments, assuring they have been made timely. The checkers should verify that these have been made so that the congregation's assets are not jeopardized. We want to fulfill our commitments – preserving the credit rating and good will of employees, creditors, and members incurring expenses.

A. Insurance premiums for property and liability coverage, as well as Errors and Omissions coverage for the trustees.

B. Workmen's compensation premiums.

C. Mortgage payments. Arrange for mortgage payments to be transferred automatically from the checking account each month. Doing this insures that the payments will be made on time each month and it decreases the expense of check processing.

D. Review the dates of payroll payments to minister and other staff against due dates. Insure that they are made on the date they are due. Cross check to the checking account, noting the date they cleared. For example, payroll checks for the 15th of the month should be dated the 15th of the month and should not clear the bank account before the 15th of the month.

E. Look for cancelled checks and receipts indicating payments to each employee's retirement fund are being made and paid timely.

F. Look at the payroll worksheets. Add the lines across and down to find errors. Compare the sums to cancelled checks. Re-compute the salaries and the taxes and compare your results to amounts on the payroll checks. If payroll tax or withholding is required on any salaries paid by the church check those payments to IRS, Social Security, and the State are being made timely.

G. Similarly, check that health insurance premiums and other employee insurance premiums are being paid on time.

H. There must be a documenting authorization process for all payments. Are bills routinely approved by persons responsible for that part of the budget? Spot check a sample of invoices. Are payments made promptly? Look at the invoice, date received, and then the date of the check. If bills are paid late routinely, or at a particular time of year, determine the reason. Trace a sample of approved invoices to the ledger and to cancelled checks showing payment. Are the amount, date, check number, and payee reconciled? Then, trace a sample of cancelled checks to the ledger and to the approved invoices. Again, are the amount, date, check number, and payee reconciled?

I. Check for duplicate payments being made. Ask for a copy of the general ledger that shows all payments made for the year by account. A scan of the ledger will show you the check amounts for each expense line. Look for repeating amounts where there should be none. If your bookkeeper is using software such as Quickbooks you can also look at a listing of all payments made to a particular vendor during the year. If something doesn't look right, check the back-up paperwork for an explanation. Even if everything looks right, spot check the back-up paperwork.

J. If the monthly financial statements compare actual against an anticipated budget amount at that point in the year (and they should), scan the accounts for those that deviate significantly. Is there a good explanation?

K. Check out each item in the Miscellaneous account. This is where many unusual items are stuck because the bookkeeper does not know where else to put them. Be sure this is where they belong.

L. While checking the payment records, also check to see if there are old (stale) checks outstanding – that is, issued but never cashed. If there are checks outstanding more than six months for example there should be some possible follow-up and/or the old checks written off.

M. Assure that any extraordinary payments to board members, staff, or finance people are adequately documented and seem reasonable.

N. Look particularly for payments made to "cash". Do these appear to be in order?

Is the income accounting process adequate, documented, and followed completely?

A. Review the written procedures for counting cash and check collections. Are the procedures and the forms complete and adequate? Can all cash be appropriately classified? Ask the bookkeeper whether they have problems deciphering how to account for receipts. Are there funds received which do not go through the regular accounting process?

B. Review the list of counting personnel and the list of record-keeping personnel. There should be no overlap in the lists.

C. Trace payments of interest and dividend income to the ledger. Do these appear to be in order?

D. Review deposit dates and amounts on bank deposit slips compared to reported dates and amounts in the accounts. Select a sample of deposits. Are there discrepancies?

E. Count the cash (usually referred to as plate collection) from the Sunday collection. A member of the Financial Review Committee should serve as an usher from time to time in order to observe the standard process for the cash count and make sure that it is actually being done. It should be done by the treasurer or his/her representative and one other person each week. Also, check the amounts verified in the cash count and match them to the weekly bookkeeping entries for the Sunday deposit. Is the plate amount the same amount? Has the treasurer shown why there is a difference on the reconciliation of deposit to payments tracking system?

F. Acknowledgement of Contributions: The IRS requires that contributors be able to produce a receipt for "any single gift" over $250. A church should produce at least an annual statement of gifts, preferably all gifts of $25 or more. If this is done the IRS requirement is met. Send out notes to 10% or more of all contributors asking whether they received such a letter, and how much the total gifts were. Compare responses to the records, looking for discrepancies.

G. Acknowledgement of Non-cash Contributions: This is a simple letter, usually issued only when requested. It acknowledges the item received (with a brief description), the purpose for which it will be used, and thanks the person. Do *not* state the value of the item; instead, include the statement, "Value is to be determined by the donor".

Are financial statements accurate?

A. Check bank statements against reports prepared for the finance committee or the board. This includes statements from checking accounts, investment funds, and any other accounts that might be set up. These accounts can be found on the balance sheet under the heading Assets or Current Assets. The bank statements balances should be reconciled routinely. Spot check the reconciliations to assure they have been done properly.

B. Verify with those who owe the church money what is the balance of the amount they owe. For example, if a previous building was sold the church could be carrying a mortgage. Check to assure that the debtor and the church have an agreed upon amortization schedule and balance owing.

C. Check the balance of loans and other liabilities on the financial statements. The most efficient way to do this is to check the year end statement. It should match exactly. Do this for any loans the church owes, including the mortgage.

D. Review copies of letters sent to those who pledge or contribute to the church. On a random basis, call or write to a few members (perhaps 10% of all members) asking them to verify that the letter kept in the church files is accurate. Verify both the total and the remaining balance. If you encounter frequent inaccuracies, expand your checking to include more members.

Are board policies followed?

A. The checkers should read board and annual meeting minutes looking for any policies that affect the financial affairs of the congregation.

B. Check that expenditures are being made in accordance with policies and resolutions of the board and congregation.

C. Check that rentals are being charged in accordance with policies. Check that users are actually paying the charges.

Report to the Board: When the review has been completed, the committee should give a written report to the board stating: what was checked, what problems, if any, were found, and what corrections or improvements are recommended for the future.

Appendix 18
Software

SOFTWARE

Unfortunately, many people take on the job of managing church finances thinking that if they keep good records of all the money coming in, and all the money going out they will have done the job. The naive volunteer may have used one of the excellent home finance software programs such as Quicken. "This has made my life easy," they say. "I could do this for the church." Such programs are well designed and are loved by many of us for the job they do in personal finance management.

Balancing your checkbook and keeping track of how you spent your money over the last six months is not the same as accounting for an organization however. Many financial transactions do not involve the checking account, as one can learn in Appendix 14 where we follow a few accounting transactions. Suppose, for example, funds are set aside for a balloon payment on the mortgage or for eventual roof replacement. Or, the board passes a policy requiring everyone with keys to the building to make a $5 deposit against possible loss. These are situations that are not easily reflected with a simple checkbook entry and will necessarily be confusing if done in that format. A report with several oddities of this sort prepared by the treasurer who "keeps everything on a spreadsheet" is soon unreadable and unreliable.

It is instructive to consider why it is that Intuit sells Quickbooks and Quickbooks for Non-Profits as well as Quicken. It is because full accounting for a small business or a United Way agency or a church is a fundamentally different task than keeping a checkbook. The issue is not that it is a *bigger* job; it is a *different* job. For those church treasurers who are trying to do church accounting with a checkbook program and a spreadsheet, I strongly recommend change. Use software designed for the job you are asked to do.

Software designed especially for use by churches can change substantially from year to year, so that it is difficult to make generalizations about how one package compares to another. And, there are many people in church offices around the country who are more familiar with software than I. What I have found over the years is that most people recommend using the package they are most familiar with. Still, the best source of insight is probably from other church treasurers in your town.

Appendix 19
Financial Statements
Report to the Board

THE COMMUNITY CONGREGATION
OPERATING BUDGET REPORT SUMMARY

	ANNUAL BUDGET	as of 12/31/2009 ANTICIP.	ACTUAL	DIFF.
OPERATING REVENUE (total)	**326,600**	**145,700**	**143,791**	**-1,909**
pledges & donations - operating support	222,900	115,200	114,486	-714
fees & sales of goods and services	42,700	1,000	668	-332
misc. income	61,000	29,500	28,637	-863
OPERATING EXPENSES (total)	**309,250**	**149,590**	**142,556**	**-7,034**
Worship & Faith Development (total)	*159,710*	*76,895*	*72,493*	*-4,402*
worship and adult learning	118,170	55,750	52,268	-3,482
children and youth programs	41,540	21,145	20,225	-920
Organiz. Devel & Operational Support (total)	*109,310*	*54,080*	*51,927*	*-2,153*
Board, training, travel	1,200	100	100	0
admin committees and Board	800	325	151	-174
office expense & misc.	6,800	3,400	4,217	817
compensation	55,000	27,500	31,150	3,650
utilities, buildings, maintenance	45,510	22,755	16,309	-6,446
Membership Growth & Support (total)	*15,230*	*6,115*	*4,683*	*-1,432*
newsletter / advertising / web	4,130	2,065	1,801	-264
membshp & hospitality	900	450	514	64
retreats & fun raisers	1,200	600	218	-382
pastoral services	9,000	3,000	2,150	-850
Community Presence / Denomination (total)	*25,000*	*12,500*	*13,453*	*953*
assistance	1,000	500	422	-78
Transylvania Church support	800	400	233	-167
denominational support	23,200	11,600	12,798	1,198
NET, CURRENT OPERATIONS	**17,350**	**-3,890**	**1,235**	**5,125**

RESERVE ACCOUNT ACTIVITY

ADDITIONS TO WORKING CAPITAL	**0**	**0**	**41,513**	**41,513**
Dedicated Income (total)	0	0	15,467	15,467
Use of Reserves (income to operating fund)	0	0	26,046	26,046
SUBRACTIONS FROM WORKING CAPITAL	**13,250**	**6,625**	**48,138**	**41,513**
Unbudgeted transfers to Reserves	0	0	15,467	15,467
Budgeted transfers to reserves	13,250	6,625	6,625	0
Use of Reserves (expense from operating fund)	0	0	26,046	26,046
NET RESERVE ACCOUNT ACTIVITY	**-13,250**	**-6,625**	**-6,625**	**0**
NET TO WORKING CAPITAL	**4,100**	**-10,515**	**-5,390**	**5,125**

THE COMMUNITY CONGREGATION
OPERATING BUDGET REPORT DETAIL

	ANNUAL	as of 12/31/2009		
	BUDGET	ANTICIP.	ACTUAL	DIFF.
OPERATING REVENUE (total)	**326,600**	**145,700**	**143,791**	**-1,909**
pledges & donations - operating support	222,900	115,200	114,486	-714
annual stewardship drive (90% of total)	206,700	108,000	106,230	-1,770
prior year recoveries (2%)	3,265	3,200	3,475	275
non-canvass pledges (5% of canvass)	10,335	2,700	3,164	464
other gifts - general support	2,600	1,300	1,617	317
sales & fees for goods and services	42,700	1,000	668	-332
workshop registrations & fees (net)	800	400	332	-68
fun raising events (net)	7,900	600	463	-137
auction (net)	34,000	0	-127	-127
misc. income	61,000	29,500	28,637	-863
endowment support	48,400	24,200	23,200	-1,000
TCC Corp.	12,600	5,300	5,437	137
OPERATING EXPENSES (total)	**309,250**	**149,590**	**142,556**	**-7,034**
Worship & Faith Development (total)	*159,710*	*76,895*	*72,493*	*-4,402*
worship and adult learning	118,170	55,750	52,268	-3,482
Minister's salary (incl. $25,000 housing)	95,300	47,650	45,400	-2,250
Minister's Professional Expenses	6,670	3,335	1,987	-1,348
Worship Committee	500	250	318	68
pulpit expenses	3,300	1,650	900	-750
music program	10,270	5,135	5,421	286
Music Committee	480	240	423	183
Music Director	6,000	3,000	3,000	0
Accompanist	3,790	1,895	1,998	103
Adult Learning & Enrichment Comm.	2,130	1,065	229	-836
A.L.E. Committee	1,130	565	140	-425
library acquisitions	1,000	500	89	-411
children and youth programs	41,540	21,145	20,225	-920
Director of Religious Education salary	34,600	17,300	16,850	-450
RE Committee	925	463	593	131
curricula, supplies, materials	3,465	1,733	1,619	-114
youth ministry	2,550	1,650	1,163	-487
Organiz. Devel & Operational Support (total)	*109,310*	*54,080*	*51,927*	*-2,153*
Board, training, travel	1,200	100	100	0
admin committees	800	325	151	-174
office expense & misc.	6,800	3,400	4,217	817
compensation	55,000	27,500	31,150	3,650
Administrator Salary	18,700	9,350	11,917	2,567
benefits & payroll taxes	36,300	18,150	19,233	1,083
utilities, buildings, maintenance	45,510	22,755	16,309	-6,446
Sexton salary	13,260	6,630	6,129	-501
mortgage interest	2,250	1,125	1,125	0
maint. supplies & svs	9,200	4,600	4,597	-3
taxes, ins, utilities	20,800	10,400	4,458	-5,942

	ANNUAL	as of 12/31/2009		
	BUDGET	ANTICIP.	ACTUAL	DIFF.
Membership Growth & Support (total)	*15,230*	*6,115*	*4,683*	*-1,432*
newsletter / advertising / web	4,130	2,065	1,801	-264
membshp & hospitality	900	450	514	64
retreats & fun raisers	1,200	600	218	-382
pastoral services	9,000	3,000	2,150	-850
Community Presence / Denomination (total)	*25,000*	*12,500*	*13,453*	*953*
assistance	1,000	500	422	-78
Transylvania Church support	800	400	233	-167
denominational support	23,200	11,600	12,798	1,198
District Contribution	3,700	1,850	2,000	150
Area Council	300	150	798	648
UUA Annual Prog Fund	19,200	9,600	10,000	400
NET, CURRENT OPERATIONS	**17,350**	**-3,890**	**1,235**	**5,125**

RESERVE ACCOUNT ACTIVITY

ADDITIONS TO WORKING CAPITAL	**0**	**0**	**41,513**	**41,513**
Dedicated Income (total)	0	0	15,467	15,467
special gifts (total)			10,546	
Sunday plate dedications			9,228	
other gifts and donations			1,318	
sales (total)	0	0	4,921	4,921
youth group wreath sales			2,136	
Sunday Soup			782	
Free Trade coffee & chocolate			423	
art gallary sales			1,580	
Use of Reserves			26,046	
SUBRACTIONS FROM WORKING CAPITAL	**13,250**	**6,625**	**48,138**	**41,513**
Unbudgeted transfers to Reserves	0	0	15,467	15,467
Budgeted transfers to reserves	13,250	6,625	6,625	0
Equity to Leave Liability Reserves	1,000	500	500	
Equity to Repair & Replacement Res.	8,000	4,000	4,000	
Equity to Sabbatical Reserves	2,000	1,000	1,000	
mortgage principal to Reserves	2,250	1,125	1,125	
Reserve spending	0	0	26,046	26,046
AIDS House			15,000	
Sunday plate collections sent			9,500	
piano repair			1,027	
new dishwasher			519	
NET RESERVE ACCOUNT ACTIVITY	**-13,250**	**-6,625**	**-6,625**	**0**
NET TO WORKING CAPITAL	**4,100**	**-10,515**	**-5,390**	**5,125**

COMMUNITY UU CHURCH
STATEMENT OF FINANCIAL POSITION

	prior 6/30/2009	current 12/31/2009
ASSETS		
Current Assets		
Petty Cash	100	100
Checking Acct	869	9,725
Saving Certificates (@ face)	68,200	50,000
Total, Current Assets	69,169	59,825
Long Term Assets		
Building (at cost)	550,000	650,000
Land (at cost)	80,000	80,000
Total, Long Term Assets	630,000	730,000
TOTAL ASSETS	699,169	789,825
LIABILITIES, RESERVES & EQUITY		
Liabilities		
mortgage	0	100,000
Less, prinicpal in reserves		-1,125
		98,875
Reserves		
unbudgeted reserves		
liturgical art & music	385	1,965
leadership development fund	414	1,196
community presence projects	687	1,110
youth group	0	2,136
Change for the World	398	126
caring & assistance fund	25,040	11,358
budgeted reserves		
sabbatical	6,295	7,295
repair & replacement	27,892	30,346
leave liability account	5,637	6,137
mortgage fund	0	2,250
subtotal, Reserves	66,748	63,919
Accumulated Equity		
beginning balance	640,763	632,421
current operations	-1,342	1,235
net reserve transfers from equity	-7,000	-6,625
Total, Accumulated Equity	632,421	627,031
TOTAL LIABILITIES, RESERVES & EQUITY	699,169	789,825

THE COMMUNITY CONGREGATION

CASH FLOWS
as of 12/31/2009

BEGINNING CASH at 6/30/2009		**69,169**
Operating Activities (net)	1,235	
plus non-cash operating expenses		
interest payments to mortgage fund	1,125	
Reserve Activities Effecting Cash		
plus income transfered to reserves	15,467	
less spending of reserves	-26,046	
NET CHANGE IN CASH		**-8,219**
ENDING CASH at 12/31/2009		**60,950**

WORKING CAPITAL CALCULATION
as of 12/31/2009

Starting Equity	632,421	**Current Assets**	60,950
less, Long Term Assets	-630,000	**less, Current Liab. & Reserves**	-63,919
Starting Working Capital	2,421	**Current Working Capital**	-2,969
Effect of Budget	4,100		
EOY Working Capital	6,521		

Appendix 20
Endowment Fund Statements

The Community Congregation

ENDOWMENT FUND
For ENDURING PROGRAMS
as of 6/30/2008

	06/30/2008
Current Carrying Value of Accounts	adjusted
Social Justice Projects	148,993
(objective met)	
Youth / Campus Ministry	31,750
$250,000 by 1/1/2012	
Art, Music & Aesthetics	15,874
$40,000 by 1/1/2010	
Economic Assistance Fund	69,884
(objective met)	
Total	266,501
Adjustments to Carrying Values since 12/31	
beginning balance	231,998
less, transfers to operating budget	-4,951
plus, additional gifts	39,454
current carrying values	266,501
Changes in Asset Values since 12/31	
Beginning Balance	231,998
Net Cash Flow	34,503
Interest & Dividends Paid	5,807
Capital Gains Realized	22,956
Net Unrealized Gains (Losses)	-10,560
Ending Balance	284,704

Appendix 21
Budget Drive Assessment

TO: Community Church Trustees
FROM: Peter Henrickson, Finance Director
SUBJECT: Perspectives on Our Annual Budget Drive

Since our recent Annual Budget Drive is complete, or nearly so, I have attached some tables displaying data about giving by our community – both historically as well as more detail on the current year. What follows are my observations about what the data suggest, and what they might mean for future budget drive efforts.

1) Those in the bottom quartile are far less likely to increase their giving level, far more likely to decrease it, and far more likely to drift away. People in this group give, individually, about 1/3 what the next higher tier gives and 1/9 what the top tier gives. Since we know we are one of the most socially/economically homogenous of all churches in the county, we cannot explain the disparity in giving as a result of income differences. This makes it clear, I believe, why we must focus only on those in the bottom quartile who have been members less than five years (about half), seeking to encourage them to become 1 – 2% contributors. After that I believe they are lost to our appeals. There are 66 households this year, of the 194 total, in which at least one person has been a member for five years or more yet the household remains in the fourth quartile. I can eyeball the list and guess that 10 – 15 are low or fixed income. The other 50 or so should be off the radar in terms of our financial expectations, in my opinion. I suggest discussion and decision by the stewardship leaders on this point. It's about ¼ of the workload, after all, when we conduct face to face canvassing.

2) In all respects the top quartile is opposite the bottom: more likely to increase; more likely to make large increases; less likely to decrease; less likely to leave.

3) Our effort to increase commitment levels this year was very successful with those who already are in the top quartile. Average stewardship commitments from that group increased 15%. Per unit levels for the bottom two quartiles did not change. The rest of the increase in stewardship income commitments resulted from new members. Next year we should focus on getting more increases from the middle quartiles.

4) For two years new families have been distributed across all quartiles. It seems that our Membership Committee under the guidance of Jean Smith has had an impact in asking for that initial stewardship commitment at the 2 – 3% level. (Amen!) We should not assume everyone "starts low and works upward over time". While that growth pattern may sometimes occur, it also seems true that many families want to manifest their place in our community by starting higher. Further, since giving at higher levels helps cement commitment to serious participation in all other aspects of congregational life, getting people to that place earlier is better than hoping they might get there later.

The Community Congregation
STEWARDSHIP DRIVE REPORT TO THE BOARD

08/09 BUDGET DRIVE SUMMARY

	waiver	4th Qrt.	3rd Qrt.	2nd Qrt.	1st Qrt.	Total
Monthly Giving Range	$0	$2 - $90	$95 - $145	$150 - $270	$275 +	
Number of HH	3	114	39	25	13	194
Total Monthly Commitment	$0	$4,659	$4,403	$4,778	$4,768	$18,608
Average (Mean)	$0	$41	$113	$191	$367	$96
Members 5+ years	1	66	28	18	16	128
New HH	0	18	5	4	3	30
Median Change (repeats)	-$27	$0	$0	$25	$20	$1
No Response during Drive		23	2	4	0	32
Dollars Lost		$872	$350	$627	$0	$1,849
Incr. $25/mo. + (repeats)	1	2	6	8	13	30
Decr. $25/mo. + (repeats)		9	4	0	0	13

HISTORICAL SUMMARY

	02/03	03/04	04/05	05/06	06/07	07/08
New HH	23	34	4	29	18	30
Total Monthly Commitment	$1,467	$1,653	$168	$1,842	$902	$1,955
Average Commitment	$64	$49	$42	$64	$50	$65
Median Commitment	$51	$30	$38	$50	$42	$48
% of Total	11%	11%	1%	11%	5%	11%
Total HH	170	203	193	192	189	194
Members 5+ years	96	115	116	115	113	128
New Commitments	23	34	4	29	18	30
No Response during Drive	39	22	15	15	22	32
HH in 1st Quartile Range	6%	6%	7%	7%	7%	7%
HH in 2nd Quartile Range	13%	12%	13%	13%	13%	13%
HH in 3rd Quartile Range	21%	19%	21%	21%	21%	20%
HH in 4th Quartile Range	60%	63%	59%	59%	58%	60%
Total Monthly Commitment	$13,837	$15,239	$16,023	$17,049	$17,448	$18,608
Average (Mean)	$82	$75	$83	$84	$92	$96
Incr. $25/mo. + (repeats)	13	20	28	19	30	30
Decr. $25/mo. + (repeats)	34	19	17	14	24	13

Note to reader:

The data in these tables was all derived by constructing a spreadsheet: list each commitment individual or family by name (put the last name in a separate column so you can alphabetize); indicate the original year one or more adults became members of the church; list the number of adult members within that household; and, list the amount of their stewardship commitment each year on a monthly basis.

Once you have done that, there are only a few spreadsheet functions one needs to learn: sort, sum, average, median, count, and simple arithmetic calculations.

The data you see here are an amalgamation of three real congregations. All the data covers the same period of time. The families were pared back randomly to get to an "average" congregation. So, what is in the table is "real" but also "not real".

One can also insert actual payments against the commitment each year. What one does with such sensitive data is certainly a key to how we each define our ministry within a congregation. I have not yet acted on the findings in my congregation. I have recently decided, however, that my task is to bring about more alignment between what people say they want to do and what they actually do. This is ministry and my pastor is helping to grapple with these issues and formulate the strategy of response.

What I think needs to happen: First, recognize that there is a small group of individuals who consistently underpay their stewardship commitment; they need to be made aware that the behavior is not anonymous; they need to know someone cares enough to pay attention to what they do. Second, this group needs to be offered the opportunity to substantially reduce the commitment they have made while we stress the importance of reliability for whatever it ends up being. Our message needs to be that predictability is more important than an unfilled hope. Third, everyone needs the opportunity at the end of each year to make good on any prior year unpaid commitment (by increasing the following year), or to formally tell us it will not be paid. Fourth, everyone needs to be offered a mechanism for automatic payment – through a debit to their bank account, for example, in order that they can more easily execute the actions they want to take.

My faith in human nature tells me that getting people who have not fulfilled their stewardship commitment in the past to deal with it responsibly in the future (no matter how small) will be good for their sense of belonging, will lead to healthier, stronger commitment to the congregation, and so will be good for them as well as the community.

BIBLIOGRAPHY

Bernstein, Leyna
CREATING YOUR EMPLOYEE HANDBOOK: A Do-It-Yourself Kit for Nonprofits
Jossey-Bass Publishers, 2000 (Includes disk with helpful draft policies and forms)

Berry, Erwin
Alban Personnel Handbook for Congregations
Alban Institute, 1999 (Includes CD with a multitude of helpful personnel management forms)
http://www.alban.org/BookStore.asp

Block, Peter
STEWARDSHIP: Choosing Service over Self-Interest
Berrett-Koehler, 1993

Callahan, Kennon L.
GIVING AND SEWARDSHIP IN AN EFFECTIVE CHURCH: A Guide for Every Member
Harper, 1992

Callahan, Kennon L.
EFFECTIVE CHURCH FINANCES: Fund Raising and Budgeting for Church Leaders
Harper, 1992

Clark, Wayne B. Ph.D.
BEYOND FUNDRAISING: A Complete Guide for Congregational Stewardship
UUA Press, 2007

Durall, Michael
THE ALMOST CHURCH, Redefining Unitarian Universalism for a New Era
Jenkin Lloyd Jones Press, 2004

Durall, Michael
BEYOND THE COLLECTION PLATE, Overcoming Obstacles to Faithful Giving
Abingdon Press, 2003

BIBLIOGRAPHY

Durall, Michael, Ed.
LIVING A CALL, Ministers and Congregations Together
Jenkin Lloyd Jones Press, 2006

Durall, Michael
CREATING CONGREGATIONS OF GENEROUS PEOPLE
Alban Institute, 1999
http://www.alban.org/BookStore.asp

Grimm, Eugene
GENEROUS PEOPLE: How to Encourage Vital Stewardship
Abingdon Press, 1992

Hammer, Richard
CHURCH AND CLERGY TAX GUIDE
Church Law Today
http://www.churclawtodaystore.com

Hammer, Richard
DOES UNRELATED BUSINESS INCOME TAX AFFECT YOUR CHURCH?
Church Law Today
http://www.churclawtodaystore.com

Hammond, Dawn
A HANDBOOK FOR CHURCH TREASURERS AND TRUSTEES
Massachusetts Conference of the United Church of Christ, 1998
http://www.macucc.org/stewardship/treasurer.pdf

Heller, Anne, et al.
CHURCHWORKS
Skinner House, 1999

Hoge, Dean R. *et al*
MONEY MATTERS: Personal Giving in American Churches
Westminster John Knox Press, 1996

Keating, Elizabeth, CPA and Peter Frumkin
"How to Assess Nonprofit Financial Performance"
Paper posted at http://ksghome.harvard.edu/~ekeatin/finassess.pdf, October, 2001

BIBLIOGRAPHY

King, Jerald L.
ASKING MAKES A DIFFERENCE
Available in the UUA Bookstore -- http://www.uua.org/bookstore

Kingman-Miller, Cecelia
"Tithing as a Spiritual Practice" in *Living a Call*, Michael Durall, Ed.
Jenkin Lloyd Jones Press, 2006

Landreth, Edward B.
FUNDRAISING WITH A VISION, A Canvass Guide for Congregations
Available in the UUA Bookstore -- http://www.uua.org/bookstore

Mead, Loren B.
MORE THAN NUMBERS: The Way Churches Grow
Alban Institute, 1998
http://www.alban.org/BookStore.asp

Miller, Herb
CONSECRATION SUNDAY STEWARDSHIP PROGRAM
Abingdon Press, 1995

Schaller, Lyle E.
44 WAYS TO EXPAND THE FINANCIAL BASE OF YOUR CONGREGATION
Abingdon Press, 1989
Vargo, Richard J.
EFFECTIVE CHURCH ACCOUNTING
Harper & Row, 1989 (Out of print and available only in used condition.)

Wuthnow, Robert
THE CRISIS IN THE CHURCHES, Spiritual Malaise, Fiscal Woe
Oxford University Press, 1997

Wuthnow, Robert
GOD AND MAMMON IN AMERICA
The Free Press, 1994

Compensation Handbook for Church Staff
A multi-denominational salary and compensation survey. Updated annually.
Find it at http://store.churchlawtodaystore.com

Made in the USA
San Bernardino, CA
03 August 2013